Praise for *Data Modeling Made Simple*

"Data Modeling Made Simple is a must read for all professionals new to data modeling as well as those that want to 'speak the language' and understand the concepts. Steve writes as though he is right there with you, walking you through the terminology, explaining the symbols, and telling you what you should consider doing before, during and after you have modeled your data."

Robert S. Seiner
President, KIK Consulting & Educational Services, LLC
Publisher, The Data Administration Newsletter, tdan.com

"Data Modeling Made Simple is an excellent training guide for anyone entering the data modeling field. Steve Hoberman takes the fundamental concepts of data modeling and presents them in an easy to understand and entertaining manner that I'm sure you will find valuable."

David Marco
President, *EWSolutions*

"How does one who is not a formally trained 'data modeler' understand the basics of data modeling? Steve Hoberman has created an informative, fun, easy to follow, and practical book sharing data modeling concepts which are essential for any professional involved in information technology. Mr. Hoberman clearly answers key questions behind the what, why and how of data modeling and reinforces the explanations with appropriate examples, analogies and exercises."

Len Silverston, Best-Selling Author of
The Data Model Resource Book, Volumes 1 and 2

Data Modeling Made Simple

A Practical Guide for
Business & IT Professionals

Steve Hoberman

Technics Publications, LLC
New Jersey
www.technicspub.com

Published by:
Technics Publications, LLC
Post Office Box 161
Bradley Beach, NJ 07720 U.S.A.
Orders@technicspub.com
www.technicspub.com

Edited by Precision Editorial Services (www.precisionedit.com)

The publisher offers discounts on this book when ordered in quantity for special sales. For more information, please contact:

Technics Publications Corporate Sales Division
Post Office Box 161
Bradley Beach, NJ 07720 U.S.A.
CorporateSales@technicspub.com

This book is printed on acid-free paper.

ISBN, print ed. 0-9771400-0-8
First Printing 2005
Printed in the United States of America

Library of Congress Control Number: 2005906929

To Dad, who taught me the value of hard work—and the even higher value of family.

Contents

Acknowledgements

I'd like to thank Jeani, Dave, and Wayne for their help with this text.

Jeani Wells is a top-notch data modeler. Her experience and ability to keep things simple had a positive influence on this text. David Wells' belief in the need for a strong relationship between business and IT helped shape this book. After conferring with him, I strove even harder to make this book relevant not only to IT experts but also to business professionals. Wayne Eckerson can make words come alive. I thank him for his insights on the text, and especially the title.

My current manager at Mars, Larry Priester, is a model manager. He knows how to motivate a team without losing sight of the individual. I thank him for his strong belief in the development of his employees.

Thanks to Craig Brelsford from Precision Editorial Services for copy-editing Data Modeling Made Simple. Thanks to Eric Dome for lending his brain on the cover. Thanks to Roger Hedden for the Cobra photo shoot.

As was the case with my first book, my wife, Jenn, worked extra hard to free up my "free" time so I could focus on writing. While I was busy writing, Jenn was busy changing diapers, mowing the grass, shopping, cleaning, and so on. I'll have to start writing again quick before that next dirty diaper comes along.

I thank my daughters, Sadie and Jamie, for reminding me to keep things simple.

I thank my dad for instilling in me a strong work ethic and a desire to understand how things tick, and my mom for setting the example of a teacher who loves to share knowledge.

Foreword

A data model is the brain of an application, a conceptual framework that represents the business as accurately as possible. It defines the players, actions, and rules that govern the ways in which business processes work, representing them in a standard syntax that both humans and applications can interpret. In essence, a data model turns business concepts into computer code so that applications and systems can process information on our behalf. Without data models, we wouldn't be able to automate many of the processes that drive our organizations.

Given the pivotal role played by data models, it should be no surprise that they often determine whether an application is effective. A poorly designed data model can wreak havoc on even the most elegantly designed application. Poor performance, inaccurate query results, inflexible rules, and inconsistent metadata are just some of the results of a poor data model. A poor data model can hamstring an application.

On the flip side, a good data model serves as a lingua franca between business and information-technology professionals. It provides a shared understanding of the business that aligns business and technical professionals at the outset of a project. Conceptual and logical data models capture the ways in which technical professionals think a business process works. Business professionals can examine those assumptions and offer corrections and refinements before code is created.

I can't think of anyone better suited to explaining how data models work in plain, simple English than Steve Hoberman. Many skilled data modelers revel in the arcane art they practice and may as well be orbiting Pluto as working with business professionals. Not so Steve, who has demonstrated a mastery of making data modeling fun and easy in the courses he teaches for The Data Warehousing Institute. Although an accomplished data modeler himself—as is evident in his other book, *The Data Modeler's Workbench*—Steve is even more skillful in connecting with his audience. His enthusiasm and energy to communicate data modeling techniques is beyond compare. Steve is one of our most beloved and effective faculty members.

Meeting an important need. I'm extremely glad that Steve has decided to write *Data Modeling Made Simple*, because the need for this kind of book is huge. Given the importance of data models to the success of applications, it is surprising that so many business people (and more than a few technical people) lack understanding about them. This book will go a long way toward raising awareness of the importance and role of data models to organizations among business and technical professionals.

Specifically, business professionals who are sponsoring an application or have been assigned to the project team will find this book a useful primer on the topic. Technical professionals who are new to application design and development will find the book a quick and easy way to learn the fundamentals of data modeling. And professors who want to help their students grasp data modeling concepts, terminology, and success criteria will want to add this book to their required reading list.

Wayne W. Eckerson
Director of Research and Services
The Data Warehousing Institute

Introduction

The writer does the most who gives his reader the most knowledge and takes from him the least time.

Charles Caleb Colton

The first book I wrote on data modeling, *The Data Modeler's Workbench,* was more than 500 pages long. I questioned how many readers read the entire book to extract all the bits of knowledge they needed to efficiently produce high-quality models. I then started thinking about those books that are most valuable to us—those books that make us want to read every chapter. Instruction manuals fit into this category. Whether for a car, digital recorder, or computer, reading the manual is almost essential to understanding how something works.

Data Modeling Made Simple was written with the same thought in mind. It is an instruction manual. In it, I provide information of immediate practical value to the reader, and I present that information as clearly and succinctly as I can. Theory and advanced topics I leave for the bigger books. Just as the instruction manual for an automobile avoids spending hundreds of pages on how an engine works, because such information is of limited use to the general reader, this book avoids spending pages on the theory, history, and mathematics behind modeling and focuses only on what is most useful.

Here are the main questions this text will answer:

- What is a data model?
- What is so special about data models?
- What are entities? What is the difference between an independent and a dependent entity?
- What are data elements? What are primary, foreign, and alternate keys?
- What are relationships and cardinality?
- What makes a definition great?
- What are the three types of subject area model?
- What is the logical data model? What are normalization and abstraction?
- What is the physical data model? What are denormalization, surrogate keys, indexing, partitioning, views, and dimensionality?
- What is the best approach to building the models? What are the top-down, bottom-up, and hybrid approaches to completing the modeling deliverables?
- How do I validate a data model? What is a scorecard?
- How do I keep my modeling skills sharp?
- What is the best data modeling tool?
- What is the future role of the data modeler?

There are more than 30 exercises throughout the text. When I teach data modeling, I rely on exercises to help reinforce concepts and keep the students alert. You will find exercises in this text for this same purpose. The more exercises you complete, the more you will get out of this book.

You will find the answers to the exercises on my Web site at www.stevehoberman.com.

CHAPTER 1: What is a data model?

I gave the steering wheel a heavy tap with my hands as I realized that, once again, I was completely lost. It was about an hour before dawn, I was driving in France, and an important business meeting awaited me. I spotted a gas station up ahead that appeared to be open. I parked, went inside, and showed the attendant the address of my destination.

I don't speak French and the attendant didn't speak English. The attendant did, however, recognize the name of the company I needed to visit. Wanting to help and unable to communicate verbally, the attendant took out a pen and paper. He drew lines for streets, boxes for traffic lights, circles for roundabouts, and rectangles for his gas station and my destination.

With this custom-made map, which contained only the information that was relevant to me, I arrived at my address without making a single wrong turn. The map was a model of the actual roads I needed to travel.

A model is a representation of something in our environment. It makes use of standard symbols that allow one to grasp the content quickly. In the map he drew for me, the attendant used lines to symbolize streets and circles to symbolize roundabouts. His skillful use of those symbols helped me visualize the streets and roundabouts.

Models are all around us. An organizational chart is a model of a reporting structure in a company. A blueprint is a model for a building. A table of contents is a model of the contents in a book. A data model, as the name makes clear, is a model of data—data that can be as complex as or more complex than those roundabouts in France.

Data, as defined by the U.K. Ministry of Defense are "A representation of facts, concepts, or instructions in a formalized manner suitable for communication, interpretation, or processing by humans or by automatic means." We not only hear the word *data* hundreds of times a day, but we encounter an almost infinite amount of data through the activities and processes in which we participate. Sometimes the sheer quantity of data is overwhelming, making even a cursory level of understanding unreachable.

I have seen many definitions for the term *data model*. Some are extremely technical, using terms such as *predicate logic* and *set theory*. Other definitions essentially say that "a data model is a model of data." Still other definitions explain not what a data model is, but what it is used for (such as the role of a data model in software development). The error is understandable. A data model is, after all, an important deliverable for any application being built on a database.

My definition of a data model is the following:

A data model is a diagram that uses text and symbols to represent groupings of data so that the reader can understand the actual data better.

A spreadsheet groups data in columns. There is a column for last name, another for first name, and so on. A data model takes this idea a step further, showing not only the column headings but also the way in which the headings relate to each other. For example, a data model will show not only "first name" and "last name," but also how first name and last name relate to each other.

A claims data model for an insurance company, for example, most likely will display claim and policy information as well as the ways in which each type of information relates to the other. Claim number, policy effective date, claim amount, deductible, and hundreds of other possible groupings of data will be diagrammed, along with the ways in which they relate to one other.

Business cards contain a wealth of data about people and the companies for which they work. In this book, we will illustrate many concepts by using a business card as a model. By building a business card data model, we will see firsthand how much knowledge we gain of the contact-management area.

I once opened the drawer in my nightstand (a scary proposition, as it had not been cleaned since the mid-1980s) and grabbed a handful of business cards. I laid them out and picked four that I thought would be the most fun to model. I chose my current business card; a business card from an internet business that my wife and I tried to start years ago when dot-com was hot; a business card from a magician who performed at one of our parties; and a business card from one of our favorite dining establishments. I changed the names and contact information to protect the innocent and reproduced these in fig. 1.1.

Fig. 1.1 Four business cards from my nightstand

Assuming our goal with this exercise is to understand the information on the business cards better, let's begin by listing some of the data:

- Steve Hoberman & Associates, LLC
- Bill Smith
- Steve
- Jenn
- FINE FRESH SEAFOOD

For the sake of brevity, let's stop here. Even though we are dealing only with four business cards, listing all the data would do little to aid our understanding. Now imagine that, instead of limiting ourselves to just these four cards, we looked through all the cards in my nightstand—or worse yet, the entire contact-management area. We would quickly become overloaded with data.

A data model groups data together to make them easier to understand. For example, we would examine the following set of data and realize that they fit within a group called "company name":

- Steve Hoberman & Associates, LLC
- The Amazing Rolando
- findsonline.com
- Raritan River Club

Taking this exercise a step further, we can organize all the data on the cards into the following groups:

- person's name
- person's title
- company name
- e-mail address
- Web address
- mailing address
- phone number
- logo (the image on the card)

So, are we finished? Is this listing of groups a data model? Not yet. We are still missing a key ingredient: the ways in which these groups relate to one other. The model will also be able to show these relationships, including showing the relationships from this conversation about the e-mail address:

Each e-mail address can be assigned to at most one person or at most one company. The e-mail address me@stevehoberman.com, for example, can be assigned only to me and no one else. On the flip side, each person or company can have zero, one, or many e-mail addresses. I actually have several e-mail addresses, and so do many people I know.

A data model for our business card example is shown in fig. 1.2. Mindful that you may not know what all the symbols in the model mean yet, I have given the figure the caption "a preview of things to come." By the time you are about halfway through this book, you should be able to understand the symbols fully.

Fig. 1.2 A preview of things to come

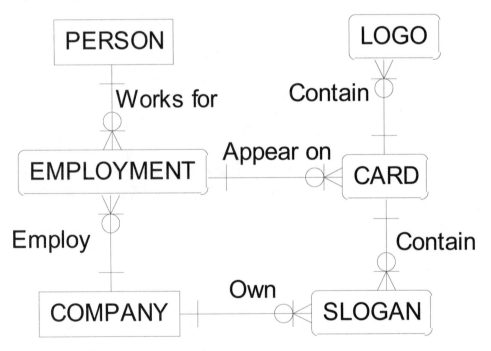

CHAPTER 2: What is so special about data models?

Traditionally, data models have been built during the analysis and design phases of a project to ensure that the requirements for a new application are fully understood and correctly captured before the actual database is created. There are, however, other uses for modeling than simply building databases. Among the uses are the following:

To understand an existing application. That is, to "reverse engineer" an application database already in production to understand its structures better.

To perform impact analysis. What is the impact of adding or modifying structures for an application already in production? How much of an application's structures is needed for archival purposes?

To understand a business area. As a prerequisite to a large development effort, it usually is necessary to understand how the business works before one can understand how the applications that support the business will work.

To facilitate training. When new team members need to come up to speed or developers need to understand requirements, a data model is an effective explanatory medium.

Rather than continue to list scenarios, let us instead understand the characteristics that make data models so invaluable. Understanding and appreciating the characteristics of modeling will help us think outside the box and come up with many creative and practical uses of data models. There are four characteristics: communication, formalization, scope, and focus. They are common not just to data models, but to models in general. We build and use data models to reap the benefits of these four valuable characteristics.

Communication

Communication is the primary reason we build data models. People who need to understand the content the models represent usually have various levels and types of experience. The model is the bridge to understanding. When the spoken word failed to reach me, the model that the gas station attendant drew for me clearly explained how to get to my destination. Regardless of whether we are trying to understand how key concepts in a business relate to one another or the workings of a 20-year-old order-processing system, the model becomes an ideal mechanism for explaining information.

I recently built a data model to capture consumer interactions with snack food. The key business user and I built a high-level model showing the subjects that are relevant for the project. The model helped with scoping the project, understanding key terms, and building a rapport with the business. This model became the mechanism with which we bridged our understandings of key terms such as *consumer*, *product*, and *interaction*. Several months later, I used a much more detailed model of the same consumer-interaction information to inform the report developers of exactly what was expected to appear on each report along with all the necessary selection criteria.

It is worth noting that companies nowadays are building fewer systems from scratch. We will continue to hear the hum of development within our organizations (building data warehouses, Web applications, customizing packaged software, Lotus Notes databases, and so on), but the hum is becoming quieter. The trend now is to buy more packaged software and to build less internally. "Reinventing the wheel" has become a dirty phrase. Years back, it was more common for the data model to lead to a database design of a brand-new application.

A new trend is emerging however, in which data models are built solely for understanding information and not with the goal of writing more code. Our roles as modelers are changing. Today, the data modeler does not simply build a new application, but he also helps organizations understand their information and the information in packaged software. Examples of this new role include modeling an entire organization to better understand the points of overlap with packaged software and creating detailed mapping documents showing how new applications map to existing applications.

The communication we derive from modeling does not begin when the data modeling phase has ended. That is, much communication and knowledge are shared during the process of building the model that can be just as valuable as the pretty picture of boxes and lines. The means are just as valuable as the ends. Let's look in more detail at the communication benefits derived both during and after the modeling process.

COMMUNICATING DURING THE MODELING PROCESS

During the process of building data models, we are forced to analyze data and data relationships. We have no choice but to acquire a strong understanding of the content of what is being modeled. Much knowledge is gained as the persons involved in the modeling process challenge each other about terminology, assumptions, rules, and concepts.

During the process of modeling an existing application that represents the recipes of manufactured items, I was amazed to witness team members with years of experience debate whether an ingredient differed from a piece of raw material. Another time, I modeled part of the logistics area as prework to building a logistics reporting application. I gained so much knowledge during this modeling process that, years later, I could still answer detailed questions on such subjects as how a bill of lading relates to a master bill of lading.

As we will witness while modeling the business card example, we will learn much about person, company, and employment information during the modeling process.

COMMUNICATING AFTER THE MODELING PROCESS

The completed data model is the medium for discussion on what to build in an application, or more fundamentally, how something works. Before I started working at a large manufacturing company, my soon-to-be manager gave me a large book containing a set of data models for the company. I read this book several times, becoming familiar with the key concepts in the business and their business rules. On my first day on the job, I already knew much about how the business worked. When my colleagues mentioned terms specific to the company, I already knew what they meant.

In our example with the business cards, we can use the model as a tool to understand how the business card industry works or to understand what needs to be built for a contact-management application, for example. Very often after a model is built, the business or application changes—but the model does not. An out-of-date model is less valuable as a communication tool. An out-of-date model also adds a "synching" step that will be required the next time the model needs to have an accurate view. Strict maintenance processes can prevent this from happening.

Formalization

Formalization means that there is a single, precise interpretation of every symbol and term on the model. The data modeling symbols representing rules can be read only one way. You might argue with others about whether the rule is accurate, but that is a different argument. In other words, it is not possible for you to view a symbol on a model and say, "I see A here" and for someone else to view the same symbol and respond, "I see B here." Going back to our example with the business card, let us stipulate that "there can be one or many phone numbers on a business card." This stipulation is imprecise, but it can be made precise on our data model, capturing assertions such as the following:

- Each business card must contain one or many phone numbers.
- Each phone number must belong on one and only one business card.

Note that once we show these assertions on the model, we might argue their validity. The question, "Why is a phone number limited just to one business card?" is an example of a pending debate after documenting this precise rule.

There are two situations however, that can degrade the precision of a data model. If the definitions behind the terms on a data model are nonexistent or poor, multiple interpretations become a strong possibility. Imagine a business rule on our model that states that an employee must have at least one benefits package. If the definition of *employee* is lacking, we may wonder, for example, whether this business rule includes job applicants and retired employees.

The second situation occurs when we introduce data that are outside the normal set of data values that we would expect in a particular data grouping. An old fashioned trick for getting around the rigor of a data model is to expand the set of values that a data grouping can contain. For example, if a rule on a model specified that a business card must have at least one phone number to exist, a clever person who wanted to get around this rule could easily expand the values of the phone numbers to include "other" or "99" or "not applicable." Such a value tied to a business card would maintain the rule that a business card have at least a single phone number, even if that phone number were really not applicable, which implies that a business card could contain zero phone numbers.

In a data model, precision is the result of applying a standard set of symbols. The traffic circles the gas station attendant drew for me were standard symbols that we both understood. There are also standard symbols used in data models, as we will discover shortly.

Scope

A data model describes a particular set of data according to the factors of time, quantity, and purpose. I like to visualize these three factors in a cube format, which I call the scope cube. See fig. 2.1.

Fig. 2.1 Scope cube

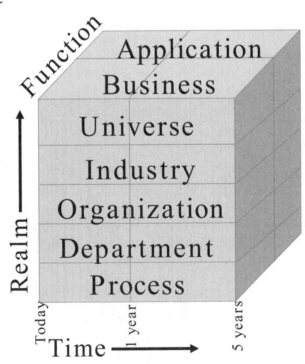

The modeler should be able to identify one point within this larger cube where the model should exist. Sometimes more than one point is identified on a given model, as when the same model is designed to show what will be different in an area five years from now as opposed to the current time.

The scope cube helps define what time, realm, and function a model contains so that we know whether the model is right and when the modeling effort is complete. If, for example, we are building a claims-processing data model to be used to build the corresponding application, the time would most likely be "today," the realm "process," and the function "application." If our model contained premium information, then our scope has expanded beyond what was originally identified on the cube.

The axis "time" shows whether we are modeling a current situation or some time in the future. I very rarely have modeled a situation that existed only in the past, so I am not including it here. I was once part of a group working on a large enterprise model, and before we started drawing boxes and lines, we determined which time view we would like. We agreed on modeling an end-of-year view as opposed to a current view, which would be quite different because the end-of-year view included a new source application with new functionality. The current view did not yet have this application.

The "realm" axis tells us what we are modeling. We can model a relatively small amount of information for a business process, such as order processing. We can model an entire department, such as sales or manufacturing. We can model our entire company, industry, or indeed the entire universe. (You can pretty much guarantee your job security by volunteering for that universe modeler position.)

The "function" axis simply shows whether the scope is an application or business area. The rules and terminology of a business area are sometimes in conflict with the application that represents it. This situation usually happens after company mergers, when one company must use the other company's application, or when a company purchases packaged software and a gap exists between how the software and business work.

You don't actually have to build one of these cubes for each of your modeling efforts. The important point is to be able to identify and gain agreement about where in each of the three dimensions you should construct your model.

Exercise 2.1

Let's apply the modeling scope cube to our example of the business card. Which factors of time, realm, and function would each of the following application efforts fit?

- A contact management application for the marketing department to be implemented in six months.
- An enterprise model of our company current view verses five years from now.
- An application for formatting business cards that currently exists.

See www.stevehoberman.com for my thoughts!

A data model can lead to intelligent decisions about program planning. Models provide a great scoping mechanism about what to develop first, second, and so on. They also highlight enhancements and hot spots. Here is an example: "The items you see in green on this data model are what we are going to develop for phase 1. Items in yellow are for phase 2, and items in red are not planned for development for the foreseeable future."

I once presented a high-level data model to a group of executives. One of them referred to the model as a "compass." This is a fitting synonym for a model, as in many cases the model's scope can help us decide where we want to go. Recall the famous conversation between Alice and the Cheshire cat in the classic, *Alice in Wonderland*, and see how a data model could have helped Alice:

Alice: I was just wondering if you could help me find my way.
Cheshire cat: Well that depends on where you want to get to.
Alice: Oh, it really doesn't matter, as long as . . .
Cheshire cat: Then it really doesn't matter which way you go.

Focus

Focus refers to the level of granularity we show on a model. A data model allows us to communicate the same content at different levels of detail. If a modeler is talking with people new to a department or high-level managers or non-technical folks, showing only the high-level concepts may be most appropriate. If you are working with analysts, database administrators, or developers, showing all the details may be most beneficial.

There are three levels of granularity for data modeling. The subject area model represents scope, the logical data model represents content, and the physical data model represents context. Here is a brief summary of each level, with many more details coming shortly:

- **Subject area model.** Also known as a conceptual or business model, the subject area model contains only the basic and critical concepts for a given scope. Here, *basic* means that it is usually mentioned a hundred times a day in normal conversation. *Critical* means that without this subject area, the department, company, or industry would be greatly changed. If we limit the scope of our example of the business card to a contact-management system, the subject areas will include *person*, *company*, and *employment*, for example.

- **Logical data model.** A logical data model is a representation of the rules behind how something works. Normalization and abstraction are the main techniques used to build the logical data model. Both techniques will be discussed shortly. The logical data model contains all the elements within our scope in a form independent of context. The context includes our environment, which consists of such things as database software, reporting tools, and usage requirements. In our business card example, we can capture that a *person* employed by a given *company* has at least one *phone number*. This relationship will be the same regardless of the type of application we are building or the software we are using.

- **Physical data model.** A physical data model is a representation, optimized for a specific context (such as software, hardware, or data), of the rules behind how something works. If, for example, we decide to build a marketing application instead of a contact-management application, although we might be using the same set of data from our business card, the resulting physical data model will be different, because the usage and tool suite will be different.

CHAPTER 3: What are entities?

An entity is something of interest to the business. *Entity* is a noun. An entity is a collection of information about something that the business deems important and worthy of capture. An entity is a who, what, when, where, why, or how. Here are some examples of each of these:

Who?	person, employee, customer, vendor, student, party, organization, department, regulatory body, competitor, subsidiary
What?	product, service, raw material, finished good, course
When?	time, date, year, calendar, fiscal period
Where?	location, address, distribution point
Why?	transaction, order, return, complaint, compliment, inquiry
How?	document, invoice, contract, agreement, account

Entity instances are the occurrences or values of a particular entity. The entity *customer* can have instances Bob, Joe, Jane, and so forth. The entity *account* can have instances for Bob's checking account, Bob's savings account, Joe's brokerage account, and so on.

An entity can be at a subject area, logical, or physical level of detail. For an entity to exist at a subject area level, it must be both basic and critical to the business. What is basic and critical depends very much on the concept of scope. At a universal level, there are certain subject areas common to all companies, such as *customer*, *product*, and *employee*. Making the scope slightly narrower, a given industry may have certain unique subject areas. *Phone number*, for example, will be a valid subject area for a telecommunications company, but perhaps not for other industries, such as manufacturing. There could be certain subject areas unique to a company or department. For example, *complaint* could be a subject area for a consumer-affairs department. *Person*, *company*, and *employment* could be valid subject areas in our example with the business card.

Exercise 3.1

Identify and define at least 10 subject areas in your organization. Make sure a few of the terms are ones that you know people debate. Try to get widespread agreement on the name and definition of each subject area.

Entities at a logical level follow the rules of normalization and abstraction, both of which will be explained shortly. Without going into a detailed explanation of normalization and abstraction at this point, we can make the general statement that a logical entity is something that can be uniquely identified with the business and has rules in the form of relationships that relate to other uniquely identified entities. In general, a subject area entity represents many logical entities. I recently constructed a subject area model in which the subject area entity *characteristic* represented more than 20 logical entities. Examining the subject area *address* in more detail could produce a large number of logical entities, including *e-mail address*, *Web address*, and *mailing address*.

At a physical level, the entities are relational database tables. The rigor applied to the logical is reversed at times to make applications perform well or to manage space more efficiently. Security, backout and recovery, and usage also become problems that we need to solve in our physical. *Web address* and *e-mail address* could be logical entities that translate directly into physical tables. However, if there is a reporting requirement to view all virtual address information, we may decide to combine both *Web address* and *e-mail address* into the same physical entity. We might also decide with very large volumes to break up *e-mail address* into several physical entities, each of a more manageable size. So at times one logical entity can break down into several physical tables, and even more frequently, one physical table can contain many logical entities.

Regardless of their level of granularity, all entities in a given data model fall into either the independent or dependent category. Note that entities are independent or dependent according to scope. *Employment*, therefore, could be dependent on *person* and *company* in our example of the business card. Note, however, that *employment* could be independent if viewed on a model without the entities *person* and *company*.

Independent

Also known as a kernel entity, an independent entity is an object of interest to the business that does not depend on any other entity for its existence. Each occurrence of an independent entity can be identified without referring to any other entity on the model. An independent entity is depicted as a rectangle. In fig. 3.1, both *person* and *company* are independent entities.

Fig. 3.1 Example of independent entities

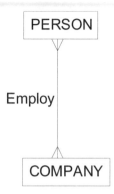

Each *person* can work for one or many *companies*.
Each *company* can employ one or many *persons*.

The model states that we don't need information about a *company* to assist in identifying a *person*, and we don't need information about a *person* to assist in identifying a *company*. Bob may be identified by *person identifier 123*, and Bob's Grocery Store may be identified by *company identifier 456*.

Dependent

A dependent entity is an object of interest to the business that depends on one or many other entities for its existence. The entities that a dependent entity depends on can be independent entities or other dependent entities. A dependent entity is depicted as a rectangle with rounded edges. There are three main types of dependent entities: attributive, associative, and category.

<u>**Exercise 3.2**</u>
Why is it important to know whether an entity is independent or dependent?

See www.stevehoberman.com for my thoughts!

ATTRIBUTIVE

An attributive entity (also known as a "characteristic" entity) depends on only one other entity: its parent entity. Part of what makes the attributive entity unique is what completely makes the parent entity unique. For example, a slogan on a business card cannot exist without the actual business card. Therefore the *slogan* is an attributive entity to *card*. See fig. 3.2.

22

Fig. 3.2 Example of an attributive entity

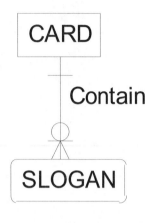

ASSOCIATIVE

An associative entity depends on two or more entities. As with the attributive entity, the associative entity is a child entity. At least part of what makes it unique comes from other entities (its parents). Uniquely identifying an instance of an associative entity requires, at a minimum, the sum of the primary keys from the participating entities.

Fig. 3.3 shows the associative entity *employment* created when the business rule between *person* and *company* states that each *person* may work for many *companies*, and each *company* can employ many *people*.

Fig. 3.3 Example of an associative entity

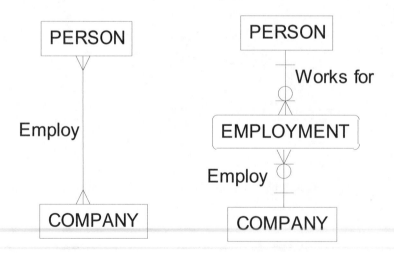

CATEGORY

Category entities are known by a number of names: subtyping, supertyping, generalization, and inheritance. I'll use the term *subtyping* throughout the text. Subtyping is grouping together the common properties of entities while retaining what is unique within each entity. The concept of subtyping can exist at subject area or logical levels of modeling. At the physical level, we need to resolve subtyping into one of several structures.

Fig. 3.4 is an example of subtyping at the subject area level in our example with the business card. *Address* can be an *e-mail address*, *Web address*, or *mailing address*. *Address* is the supertype, and *e-mail address*, *Web address*, and *mailing address* are the subtypes. We'll explore this example in more detail at the logical and physical levels in future sections.

Fig. 3.4 Subtyping example at a subject area level

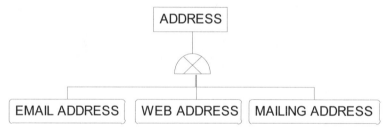

The subtyping relationship exists between the supertype and each of its subtypes. There is no relationship implied by the subtyping symbol between the subtypes, except insofar as these subtypes share the same set of properties. If there is a relationship between *e-mail address* and *Web address*, it will need to be shown as well. The subtyping relationship implies that all the properties from the supertype are inherited by the subtype. In addition to its own properties, *e-mail address* also has those of *address*.

Two types of subtypes are used in the information engineering (IE) notation, which is the modeling notation we are using throughout the text: non-overlapping and overlapping. *Non-overlapping*, or *exclusive*, means that an instance of an entity supertype can be any of the subtypes but cannot be more than one of them. *Overlapping*, or *inclusive*, means that an instance of an entity supertype can be one or many of the subtypes. See fig. 3.5 for both of these variations.

Fig. 3.5 Non-overlapping versus overlapping subtypes

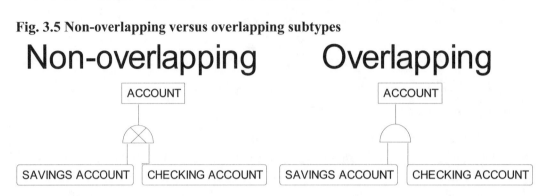

The subtyping symbol on the left with an *X* within it represents non-overlapping. This is the default in the information engineering notation, and therefore the most frequently occurring. An *account* can be a *savings account* or a *checking account*, but not both. In the second example, the subtyping symbol without the *X* represents overlapping: an *account* can be a *savings account*, a *checking account*, or both. When the subtype is overlapping, therefore, Bob could have an account with the characteristics of both a savings and a checking account.

Let's have just one more bit of fun before we leave the subtyping topic and the topic of independent and dependent entities. Fig. 3.6 contains a data model using subtyping to show the relationships between the various types of entities.

Fig. 3.6 Various types of entities

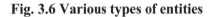

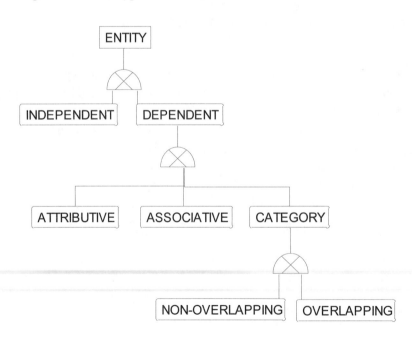

An *entity* is either an *independent* or *dependent* entity. If an entity is *dependent*, it is either an *attributive*, *associative*, or *category* entity. If it is a *category* entity, it is either *non-overlapping* or *overlapping*.

I chose to use non-overlapping subtype symbols in fig. 3.6 because I am limiting my scope to a single model. As I mentioned earlier, an entity can be dependent on one model and independent on another. If I had been representing all possible models in fig. 3.6, I would have chosen an overlapping subtype. For example, *Web address* is a dependent entity in fig. 3.4, but it could very well be an independent entity in another data model, such as one depicting internal departments and their many intranet sites.

Exercise 3.4

For which types of applications is subtyping most useful? For which types is it least useful?

See www.stevehoberman.com for my thoughts!

CHAPTER 4: What are data elements?

A data element is a property of importance to the business whose values contribute to identifying or describing instances of an entity. The term *data grouping*, used earlier in the text, is a synonym for a data element. The data element *student last name*, for example, describes the last name of each student. The data element *gross sales amount* describes the monetary value of a transaction. The data element *claim number* uniquely identifies each claim.

The part of the definition about the importance to the business means that within a certain scope or group of interest, the property must be deemed important to be considered a data element. *Logo* and *slogan*, for example, may be valued by an advertising agency but may very well be ignored as data elements by a telemarketing company that may require only *name* and *phone number*.

As with entities, data elements can exist at subject area, logical, and physical levels. A subject area must be a concept both basic and critical to the business. We do not usually think of data elements as subject areas, but they can be subject areas. When I worked for a telecommunications company, *complete telephone number* was a data element so important to the business that it was represented as a subject area on a number of high-level subject area models.

A data element on a logical data model is atomic and at times generic. *Atomic* means that the data element contains one and only one piece of business information and cannot be broken down any further. For example, we would not have one logical data element containing city, state, and zip code, but three. The process of normalization would have imposed this rule. *Generic* means that when there is a need for additional flexibility, we create more encompassing data elements. In our example with the business card, we may decide to have data elements called *phone number* and *phone type code* that can represent different types of phone numbers, such as fax and mobile. We may decide to have a *party name* instead of a *person name* and a *company name*. We may decide to have a *postal code* instead of a *zip code*.

I use the term *data element* throughout the text for consistency, but there are, depending on context, more appropriate names for the characteristics of an entity. *Element* is usually reserved for a property at an atomic level. (You cannot break the property down into smaller pieces.) *Complete phone number*, for example, is not an element, because it contains *country code*, *area code*, and *phone number*—each distinct atomic elements.

If the context is viewed through the eyes of a business person, the term *attribute* is most appropriate. If the business person views them distinctly as an entity property, *complete phone number* and *area code* could be attributes.

Column or *field* are the terms used when referring to a property of the entity specific to the database. This is how the data element is represented in the actual database software. For the most part, one column contains one or many atomic elements. *Area code* may translate directly into the physical column AREA_CD. This is a one-for-one translation from element to column. *Country code*, *area code*, and *phone number* may translate into the physical column COMPLETE_PHONE_NUM. This is a many-to-one translation from element to column.

When a subject area model contains data elements, the elements are usually attributes and rarely also elements. A logical data model generally contains nothing but elements. A physical data model contains exclusively columns or fields. Throughout the text you will see the term *data element*.

Domain

The complete set of all possible values that a data element contains is called a domain. A data element never can contain values outside of its assigned domain, which is defined by specifying the actual list of values or a set of rules. *Employee gender code*, for example, is limited to the domain of (*female*, *male*).

Employee hire date initially can be assigned the rule that its domain contain only valid dates, for example. Therefore, this can include values such as

- `February 15th, 2005`
- `25 January 1910`
- `20030410`
- `March 10th, 2050`

Because *employee hire date* is limited to valid dates, it does not include February 30th, for example. We can restrict a domain with additional rules. For example, by restricting the *employee hire date* domain to dates less than today's date, we would eliminate March 10th, 2050. By restricting *employee hire date* to YYYYMMDD (that is, year, month, and day concatenated), we would eliminate all the examples given except for 20030410. Another way of refining this set of values is to restrict the domain of *employee hire date* to dates that fall on a Monday, Tuesday, Wednesday, Thursday, or Friday (that is, the typical workweek).

In our example with the business card, *name* may contain thousands or millions of values.

The values from our four sample cards would be

- Steve Hoberman
- Steve
- Jenn
- Bill Smith
- Jon Smith
- John Doe

The *name* domain may need a bit of refining. It may be necessary to clarify whether a valid domain value can be composed both of a first and last name, such as "Steve Hoberman." Note that these values could lead to data redundancy if *Steve Hoberman* and *Steve* denote the same person.

Defining domains, assigning domains to data elements, and enforcing valid domain values ensure a level of data quality that would not be possible if we allowed a data element to contain just any value. Imagine the chaos that would result from allowing employees to be assigned hire dates of "January 35th, 2009," "cat," and "dog."

Exercise 4.1

Part A:

What do you think the domains for the following three data elements should be?

- e-mail address
- Web address
- telephone number

Part B:

Now that you have domains defined for each of the foregoing three data elements, assume you are project manager for an application that will be populating these three data elements. In your application, how would you like to see domain violations handled? In other words, if an e-mail address arrives that does not belong to the domain you defined for e-mail addresses, what kind of action would you like to see taken? Why?

See www.stevehoberman.com for my thoughts!

Keys

A data element becomes a key or non-key upon assignment to an entity. A key data element partly or fully identifies an entity instance, and/or partly or fully references a unique instance from another entity. By *partly*, I mean that a data element is part of a key, in which case there is more than one data element that makes up the entire key. The term *composite key* is used when there is more than one data element that makes up the key. Non-key data elements include all those that are not a key or part of a key, such as *Web address* and *logo*.

A candidate key represents the one or many data elements that uniquely identify a value in an entity. Candidate keys are either primary or alternate keys. A primary key represents the one or more data elements that uniquely identify a value in an entity and that is chosen to be *the* unique identifier, as opposed to an alternate key that also uniquely identifies entity occurrences but is not chosen as the unique key. Both primary and alternate keys must be unique, minimal, and stable (that is, the values can't change over time).

The reason for selecting one unique identifier over another (that is, designating one set of data elements as the primary key and another set as the alternate key) is efficiency. The primary key needs to facilitate fast navigating of tables and should take up minimal space. Alternate keys tend to embody what the business feels is truly unique about the entity.

In our example with the business card, the combination of *person's name*, *company name*, and *phone number* could make a candidate key for a particular contact. So *Steve Hoberman*, *Steve Hoberman & Associates, LLC*, and *212-555-1212* identify me as a unique contact. This candidate key may be more appropriate as an alternate key instead of a primary key, because of the inefficiency and instability inherent in having three relatively long string data elements make a contact unique. Making these data elements an alternate key will lead to adding a fabricated data element such as contact identifier as the candidate key that is chosen as the primary key. This fabricated key is known as a surrogate key.

A surrogate key is a unique identifier of a table. A surrogate key is an integer whose meaning is unrelated to its face value. (In other words, you can't look at a month identifier of 1 and assume that it represents January.) The surrogate key is usually a system-generated counter. In almost all cases, surrogate keys are not visible to the business. They remain behind the scenes to help maintain uniqueness, allow for more efficient navigation across structures, and facilitate integration across applications. In the section on physical data modeling, we will discuss surrogate keys at greater length.

A foreign key is a data element that provides a link to another entity. When a relationship is created between two entities, the entity on the "many" side of the relationship inherits the primary key from the entity on the "one" side of the relationship. (This sentence will make more sense after you have read the next section.) The foreign key allows for navigation between structures.

Let's tie this discussion on keys together with an example. Within a university environment, there is an entity called *student grade* that stores the grade received for each student for each class for a particular semester. Some sample values appear in table 4.1.

Table 4.1. Sample values for STUDENT GRADE

Class Identifier	Student Identifier	Semester Identifier	Final Grade
123	44	39	C
45	44	39	B
123	32	39	B
123	44	40	A

What makes each row in *student grade* unique? The candidate key is *class identifier*, *student identifier*, and *semester identifier*. This is also the primary key. *Class identifier* is part of the primary key and also appears to be a surrogate key. *Class identifier* most likely points to *class*, which contains a description of each class. Therefore, *class identifier* "123" can point back to the instance "Biology 101" in *class*. Therefore, *class identifier* is also a foreign key. The same explanation goes for *student identifier* and *semester identifier*. For example, the student Bob Smith may have received a C in Biology 101 in his freshman year (the first row), and retaken this class in his senior year and received an A (the fourth row).

Exercise 4.2

In the following entity, which data elements would make a good alternate key?

TAXPAYER

Taxpayer Identifier
First Name
Last Name
Social Security Number
Federal Tax Id Number
Company Name
Address Line 1 Text
City Name
State Name
Zip Code

See www.stevehoberman.com for my thoughts!

CHAPTER 5: What are relationships?

In its most general sense, a rule is an instruction about how to behave in a specific situation. The following are examples of rules that we have set or rules that have been set for us:

- Your room must be cleaned before you can go outside and play.
- If you get three strikes, you are out and it is the next batter's turn.
- The speed limit is 55 mph.

When we build an application, setting rules means defining constraints on what the application (and therefore the user) can and cannot do. At the highest level, a rule can be either a data rule or an action rule. Data rules are instructions on how data relate to one another. Action rules are instructions on *what* to do when data elements contain certain values.

There are both structural and referential integrity (RI) data rules. Structural rules (also known as cardinality rules) define the quantity of each entity instance that can participate in a relationship. For example:

- Each product can appear on one or many order lines.
- Each order line must contain one and only one product.
- Each student must have a unique student number.

RI rules focus on ensuring valid values:

- An order line cannot exist without a valid product.
- A claim cannot exist without a valid policy.
- A student cannot exist without a valid student number.

Action rules are instructions on *what* to do when data elements contain certain values:

- Freshman students can register for at most 18 credits a semester.
- A policy must have at least three claims against it to be considered high-risk.
- Take 10% off an order if the order contains more than five products.

In our data models, we can represent and enforce data rules, yet for the most part only represent the data to support action rules. That is, we cannot enforce action rules on a data model. Note that there are always exceptions, and the creative modeler can leverage subtyping or database views (which we will discuss shortly) to represent and enforce a subset of action rules. Using subtyping to enforce action rules has its pros and cons, and is outside the scope of this text. There are, however, several examples of how to leverage subtyping within the design challenges on my Web site at www.stevehoberman.com.

Exercise 5.1

Which of the following rules can be represented on a data model?

a) An order is identified by an order number and must have a valid ID from a customer and salesperson.
b) A high-risk property is one that has had three or more claims filed in the last four years with a total value of more than $50,000 in losses.
c) Monthly sales reports can be produced only for managers and senior managers.
d) A policy can be either active or inactive.
e) A bill of materials must contain at least five ingredients.
f) If you receive three speeding tickets, then you lose your driver's license.

See www.stevehoberman.com for my thoughts!

Rules are visually captured on our data models through relationships. A relationship describes both the structural and integrity rules between two entities. Because entities can be explained at three levels of granularity, the relationships that connect entities can also be shown at the subject area, logical, and physical levels of detail.

In our example with the business card, *person* and *company* were among the subject area entities we defined. If a relationship exists between *person* and *company*, both a structural and RI component are implied. The structural component could be, "Each *person* can work for many *companies*, and each *company* can employ many *people*." The RI component could be, "A *person* can exist without working for a *company*, but a *company* cannot exist unless there is at least one *person*." Both the structural and RI components of this relationship can be combined to read

Each *person* can work for zero or many *companies*.
Each *company* must employ one or many *persons*.

Logical entities that are governed by normalization and abstraction are connected by more specific rules, such as showing the various components of a person's address as separate entities according to the relationships among the address data elements.

The relationships connecting physical entities are called database constraints. An example of a constraint would be not allowing a *company* to be created unless at least one *person* is employed there.

Cardinality

Cardinality represents the symbols on both ends of a relationship that define the number of instances of each entity that can participate in the relationship. It is through cardinality that the data rules are captured and enforced. Without cardinality, the most we can say about a relationship is that two entities are connected in some way through a rule. For example, *person* and *company* have some kind of relationship, but we don't know much more than this.

The domain of values to choose from to represent cardinality on a relationship is limited to three values: zero, one, or many. *Many* (some people read it as *more*) means any number greater than one. We can't specify an exact number (other than through documentation), as in "A car has four tires." We can only say, "A car has many tires."

Each side of a relationship can have a combination of zero, one, or many. Through the specification of one or many, the structural portion of the cardinality represents the quantity of each entity instance in the relationship. The RI portion of the cardinality focuses on ensuring valid values through the specification of zero or one.

Each of the cardinality symbols are illustrated through the following example of *product* and *order line*. A product is something that an organization sells in the hope of making a profit. An order line exists for each product on a particular order. For example, an order for five widgets and two doodads would mean two order lines in one order, with each order line tying back to a particular product. Formalizing the rules between product and order line, we have

Each *product* can appear on one or many *order lines*.
Each *order line* must contain one and only one *product*.

Fig. 5.1 captures these business rules.

Fig. 5.1 *Product* and *order line*, take 1

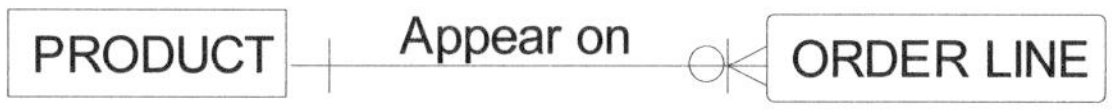

PRODUCT —|— Appear on —o<— ORDER LINE

You need to know only three symbols to read any relationship. The small vertical line means "one." The circle means "zero." The triangle with a line through the middle means "many." Some people call the "many" symbol a *crow's foot*. The label ("Appear on") on the line in this example helps in reading the relationship and understanding the rule that the relationship represents.

Every relationship has a parent and child. The parent entity appears on the "one" side of the relationship, and the child appears on the "many" side of the relationship. When you read a relationship, it is a good practice to start on the "one" side, because the entity there is typically the more independent of the two entities and sometimes provides a context for the child entity. Starting with the parent also adds consistency when interpreting the rules.

We use the word *each* in reading each relationship, starting with the parent side.

The relationship in fig. 5.1 is therefore read as follows:

Each *product* can appear on zero, one, or many *order lines*.
Each *order line* must belong to one and only one *product*.

This relationship most closely matches the original business rule that we talked about several paragraphs earlier. Let's change the cardinality slightly between these two entities and read the resulting business rules.

Fig. 5.2 *Product* **and** *order line*, **take 2**

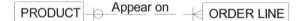

Fig. 5.2 is interpreted as follows:

Each *product* can appear on one or many *order lines*.
Each *order line* can belong to zero or one *product*.

Fig. 5.3 *Product* **and** *order line*, **take 3**

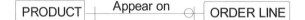

Fig. 5.3 is interpreted as follows:

Each *product* can appear on zero or one *order line*.
Each *order line* can belong to one and only one *product*.

Fig. 5.4 *Product* and *order line*, take 4

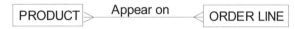

Fig. 5.4 is interpreted as follows:
Each *product* can appear on one or many *order lines*.
Each *order line* can belong to one or many *products*.

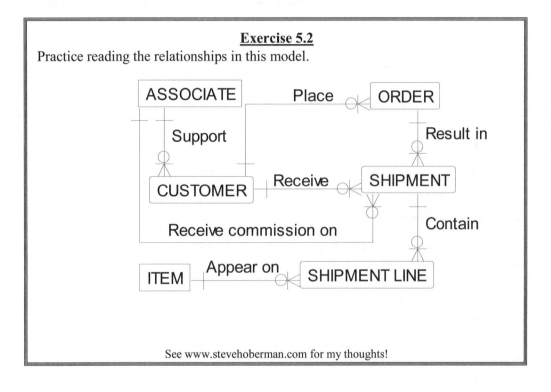

Recursion

A recursive relationship is a rule that exists between instances of the same entity. Although recursive relationships are very flexible structures, they can be complex and confusing for project teams—especially users. An example of a recursive relationship appears in fig. 5.5.

Fig. 5.5 *Product* recursive relationship, take 1

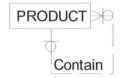

Fig. 5.5 is interpreted as follows:

Each *product* may contain zero, one, or many other *products*. A chocolate bar, for example, can contain sugar, cocoa, and milk.

Each *product* may be part of zero or one other *product*. So for example, sugar can belong to at most one other product, such as a chocolate bar.

I use sample values to validate cardinality. In the second rule above, it is not realistic to assume that sugar belongs to just one product. Sugar can belong to many products. I usually try to find examples of actual data that don't support the cardinality. If the cardinality is wrong and I detect the mistake early, then I can repair it easily. If you cannot think of any examples that contradict the cardinality, then the cardinality is most likely correct. See table 5.1 for sample relationship instance values for fig. 5.5.

Table 5.1 Sample relationship instance values for fig. 5.5

Chocolate bar	sugar
Chocolate bar	cocoa
Chocolate bar	milk
Chocolate bar	peanuts
Chocolate bar	preservatives

Recursive relationships represent several levels of rules. For example, fig. 5.5 can represent the complex bill-of-materials structure. Each relationship instance represents one link in the bill-of-materials hierarchy. *Chocolate bar* and *sugar* form one link in the hierarchy.

An employee reporting organization is another example of a recursive relationship that forms a hierarchical structure, because the recursive relationship itself is a one-to-many relationship. In an employee reporting organization, each entity instance represents one link in the hierarchy. One relationship instance will capture that Bob works for Mary. Another relationship instance builds on this and captures that Mary works for Jane.

Recursive relationships can also form network structures, as in fig. 5.6. Here, the relationship is many-to-many, which most likely more accurately represents the true business rule. Sugar, for example, can belong to many products, not just chocolate bars. Network structures lead to even more complicated relationships between entity instances than hierarchies. Hierarchies can stipulate that a single parent is assigned to one child, but networks allow children to be assigned to more than one parent.

Fig. 5.6 *Product* recursive relationship, take 2

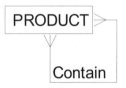

Fig. 5.6 is interpreted as follows:

Each *product* may contain zero, one, or many other *products*. For example, a chocolate bar may contain sugar, cocoa, and milk.
Each *product* may be part of zero, one, or many other *products*. For example, sugar may be part of a chocolate bar or a lollipop.

Data modelers have a love-hate relationship with recursion. On the one hand, recursion makes modeling a complex structure a relatively painless procedure. On the other hand, some consider using recursion to be taking the easy way out of a difficult modeling situation. There are many rules that can be obscured by recursion. *Bill of materials*, for example, contains many complex rules that could lead the modeler to subtype *product* into *raw material*, *ingredient*, and so on, and show all the rules between these entities. Those in favor of recursion argue that you may not be aware of all the rules and that recursion protects you from having an incomplete model. The recursion adds in a level of flexibility that ensures that any rules not previously considered are also handled by the model. It is therefore wise to consider recursive on a situation-by-situation basis.

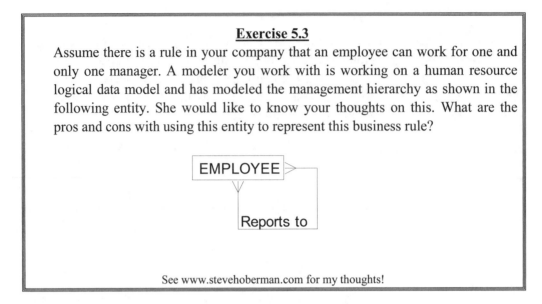

Exercise 5.3

Assume there is a rule in your company that an employee can work for one and only one manager. A modeler you work with is working on a human resource logical data model and has modeled the management hierarchy as shown in the following entity. She would like to know your thoughts on this. What are the pros and cons with using this entity to represent this business rule?

EMPLOYEE

Reports to

See www.stevehoberman.com for my thoughts!

Identifying and non-identifying relationships

A relationship is either identifying or non-identifying. An identifying relationship means that one of the participating entities is a dependent entity. That is, one of the entities is at least partly dependent upon the other entity for its identification. We cannot identify the child entity without using, at least in part, the parent's primary key. This type of relationship is shown with a solid line. Fig. 5.7 revisits the *product* and *order line* relationship, which is an identifying relationship.

Fig. 5.7 Example of an identifying relationship

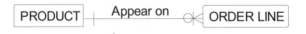

PRODUCT — Appear on — ORDER LINE

Order line cannot be identified without a *product*, and is therefore dependent on *product*. If *order line* is a dependent entity only on *product*, we would have a good example of an attributive entity (discussed earlier). Note the rounded corners on the *order line* entity. This relationship means that at least part of the *order line*'s primary key is the primary key from *product*. For example, the primary key to *order line* could be *product identifier* and *order line sequence number*.

In a non-identifying relationship, the child entity does not need the parent entity's primary key for its identification. It still may be mandatory that the child contain the parent's primary key, but it is not identifying. This type of relationship is shown with a dotted line. See fig. 5.8 for an example.

Fig. 5.8 Example of non-identifying relationship

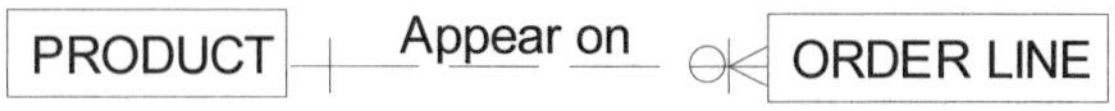

The dotted line connecting the two entities means that the *order line* contains a foreign key back to *product*, but it is not an identifying relationship, and the foreign key from *product* is, therefore, not a part of *order line*'s primary key. So for example, the primary key to *order line* could be just *order line sequence number*, and a non-identifying foreign key would be *product identifier*.

Relationship labels

Labels are the verbs that appear on the relationship lines. Labels allow us to describe a rule directly on the model. Labels should be as descriptive as possible. Here are some examples of good label names:

-   contain
-   work for
-   own
-   initiate
-   categorize
-   apply to

Always avoid the following words as label names, as they provide no additional information to the reader (you can use these words in combination with other words to make a meaningful label name; just avoid using these words by themselves):

-   has
-   have
-   associate
-   participate
-   relate
-   be

For example, replace the relationship sentence

A *person* is associated with one *company*.

With

A *person* is employed by one *company*.

I find myself sometimes using these generic words as labels when I am not paying close enough attention to the relationship. As hard as it might be, it is important to replace these generic words with words that are relevant and more descriptive to the particular business rule. If you find your model is too large to show the labels, you may decide to hide them and show them only when creating smaller subsets of the model.

Exercise 5.4

To illustrate the importance of specifying labels on relationships, think of at least five appropriate labels that could apply to this relationship.

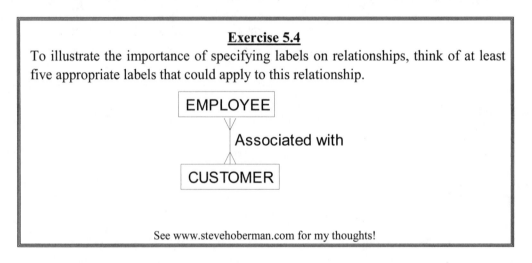

See www.stevehoberman.com for my thoughts!

CHAPTER 6: What makes a definition great?

I was sitting at a table in a meeting room, listening to managers describing their projects. Although this meeting was part of a celebration of the success of a very large data warehouse project, this part of the meeting was dedicated to lessons learned. Each manager was talking about what he would have liked to have done if he'd had the opportunity to do it all over again. I jotted down the keywords from each of the presentations. Looking over my notes afterward, I noticed a common theme: Each manager wished that he had put more effort into documenting the meanings behind the terms in his applications.

Why is documenting meanings important? More specifically, why is accurate documentation of data-element and entity definitions important? There are three main reasons. We'll use this data model from fig. 5.8 to illustrate each of them:

PRODUCT —— Appear on —◁ ORDER LINE

- **To support the rigor on the data model.** As we can see in this example, where each *order line* must be for one and only one *product*, a data model is exact and unambiguous. An *order line* cannot exist without a *product*. However, if the definition of *product* is missing or vague, we have less confidence in the entity and its relationships. Is a *product*, for example, raw materials and intermediate goods, or only a finished item ready for resale? Can we have an order for a service, or must a *product* be a tangible deliverable? The definition is needed to support the *product* entity and its relationship to *order line*.

- **To assist technology professionals in making intelligent development decisions.** How do we know which data element to source data from, to use in calculations, or to display to the user? We can look at sample data and the names of the data elements, but we lean most heavily on the definition. If the definition of *order line* mentions that open orders, canceled orders, and dropped orders are also within the scope of *order line*, this might influence sourcing decisions and database design decisions if space and performance become issues.

- **To assist business professionals in making intelligent business decisions.** In the good old days, definitions were always behind the scenes, only to be used by technical staff occasionally when validating data elements. However, with business intelligence and data warehousing pushing data elements to the very screens and reports of business people, the definitions help confirm that the right field has been chosen. They also reduce misunderstandings. A business-intelligence project can be developed flawlessly, but if a business person has a different interpretation of a data element than what was developed, it is easy for poor decisions to be made, compromising the entire application. If a business person would like to know how many products have been ordered each month, for example, imagine the poor judgments that could result if the person expected raw materials to be included with products and they were not, or if he or she assumed that raw materials were not included but they were.

You will find that many of the misinterpretations of entities and data elements stem from a difference in state. Entities travel through different states in their life cycles, and a big point of confusion is interpreting an entity as meaning only one of its states or different states that are not intended. Thinking that *product* contains raw materials (raw materials being but one state in the product life cycle), or that *order* contains open orders (open orders being but an early state in the order life cycle), lead to frequent communication gaps. Definitions can nip these problems in the bud.

Despite their importance, definitions tend to be omitted or written with minimal attention to their audience. Therefore, when writing definitions, we need to be aware of three characteristics that lead to a high-quality definition that the audience can understand. Those characteristics are clarity, completeness, and accuracy. I'll summarize them in this section. Please refer also to another book of mine, *The Data Modeler's Workbench*, for an entire chapter dedicated to definitions.

Clarity

Clarity means that a reader can understand the meaning of a term by reading the definition only once. A clear definition does not require the reader to decipher how each sentence should be interpreted. A good way to make sure your definition is clear is to think about what makes a definition unclear. We need to avoid restating the obvious and using obscure technical terminology and abbreviations in our definitions. Just to restate the obvious, *restating the obvious* means that we are not providing any new information. We are merely describing something that already has been mentioned or that is easy to find elsewhere. Let's say, for example, that the definition of *associate identifier* is "associate identifier" or "the identifier for the associate." Equally unclear is the use of synonyms, as in the pseudo definition "the identifier for an employee." As far as clarity is concerned, we also need to make sure our audience understands the terms in our definition. Using acronyms, abbreviations, and industry jargon in definitions without explaining them can cause one to lose some of one's audience.

Completeness

This category focuses on making sure the definition is at the appropriate level of detail and that it includes all the necessary components, such as derivations and examples. Having a definition at the appropriate level of detail means that it is not too generic as to provide very little additional value, yet not so specific that it provides value only to an application or department—or that it adds value only at a certain point in time.

Sometimes, in order to meet the needs of the entire company (or even the entire industry), we create a very generic definition so that all parties can agree on the meaning. It is usually a very short definition, one that does not offend any of the parties. It is a definition that leaves little to debate, because it meets everyone's needs at a high-level. Generic definitions can include dictionary quotations, ambiguous terminology, and the omission of units of measure or of derivations.

An example of a dictionary quotation as a definition for *product* might be "something produced by human or mechanical effort or by a natural process." What value does this dictionary quotation provide for an organization? If this dictionary quotation is *part of the* definition instead of *being* the definition, the definition might be considered complete.

An example of an ambiguous terminology definition for Social Security number might be "associated with an employee." We know the Social Security number is associated with an employee, but what does it mean?

An example of a definition containing an omission would be this hypothetical definition of *order weight*: "the total shipping weight of an order delivered to a destination, including packaging, that is used to ensure that the maximum carry weight on a truck is not exceeded." It is not clear from this definition whether the order weight is in pounds, hundred weight (hundreds of pounds), tons, or tonnes (metric tons).

The opposite of making a definition too generic is making it too specific. "Too specific" means that the definition is correct within a certain scope but does not address the complete scope implied by the term being defined. Definitions that are too specific usually include references to certain departments, applications, or states. Sometimes they simply include examples or derivations. For example, imagine if the definition of the term *party* included only examples:

```
customer
supplier
competitor
employee
```

Examples alone make for an incomplete definition. For a definition to be complete, the broadness of the definition must match the broadness of the term.

Accuracy

This category focuses on having a definition that completely matches what the term means and is consistent with the rest of the business. *Accuracy* means that an expert in the field would agree that the term matches the definition. One of the difficulties with this category is that as we define broader terms that cross departments, such as *product*, *customer*, and *employee*, we tend to get more than one accurate definition, depending on who is asked. A recruiting department, for example, may have a definition for *employee* that is accurate but nonetheless different from the definition offered by a benefits department. The problem is the state issue, discussed earlier. A good solution to this problem is to use subtypes on your model that contain each of the distinct states of an employee. Through the accurate definition of each subject, every state is captured.

Exercise 6.1

A modeler was having a difficult time getting three departments to agree on a definition of *student*. She eventually looked up *student* in the dictionary and suggested that they use this definition:

```
Any individual for whom an educational institution main-
tains educational records.
```

What are the pros and cons of sticking with this dictionary definition?

See www.stevehoberman.com for my thoughts!

CHAPTER 7: What is the subject area model?

Also known as a conceptual or business model, the subject area model is a visual containing a high-level perspective on something of importance to the business. It contains only the basic and critical concepts within a given realm for either a business or application function. A realm, as mentioned in the scope cube discussion in chapter 2, can be a process, a department, an organization, an industry, or even the universe. Due to the possibility of a subject area model's covering a very broad area, it is imperative to model at the right level of granularity.

In our example with the business card, a basic and critical concept is *address*, but so is *mailing address*. In a subject area model, should we have a box for *address*, only *mailing address*, or both? The key with subject area modeling is to model at a level detailed enough that we are touching business complexity.

Touching business complexity means modeling at a level where the audience and modelers can truly benefit from the content. This may sound like a vague statement, so let me illustrate it with an example. During one of my training classes, three groups are working through subject area modeling exercises. The first group finishes its model in less than 10 minutes, and there is very little discussion or debate. The second group spends the entire length of the exercise debating how to uniquely identify one of the subject areas. The third group is debating the distinction between two business concepts that sound very similar, and it is using examples to decide their fate.

The first group has a model that may be correct, yet is probably much too vague to add value. Taking up our example with the business card again, such a vague model may resemble fig. 7.1.

Fig. 7.1 A subject area model that is too vague

- Each *party* may contain many *communications*, such as a phone number or mailing address.
- Each *communication* may belong to one or more *parties*.

This model is obviously a complete model, as it accommodates all these scenarios:

- Bob can have a main phone number, fax number, and mailing address.

- The same mailing address that belongs to Bob can also belong to Mary.
- Bob's Plumbing can have the same mailing address as Bob.

Revisit the four business cards earlier and find out whether this model can accommodate everything on them. I believe the answer will be yes. This kind of model is complete, but we are not touching business complexity.

Exercise 7.1

Are there any situations in which a generic model such as in the one in fig. 7.1 would be useful?

See www.stevehoberman.com for my thoughts!

Of the three groups in the previous example, the first group's model is too generic and the second group's model is too detailed. As soon as I hear such words as *key*, *indexes*, and *partitions*, I know the group is jumping ahead to more detailed models without first understanding the subject areas. Only the third group, which is tackling distinctions between business concepts, appears to be at the right level.

There are three types of subject area models that I use often, and I've coined acronyms for them that are easy to remember: the business subject area model (BSAM), the application subject area model (ASAM), and the comparison subject area model (CSAM).

Business subject area model (BSAM)

The BSAM is a subject area model of a defined portion of the business. The scope can be limited to a department or function such as manufacturing or sales. It can be as broad as the entire company or industry. Company models tend to include external concepts such as government agencies, competitors, and suppliers. The BSAM focuses on a business area, not a particular application.

Here are some examples of BSAMs:
- A model for a large university showing a single view of *person* and how the roles a person plays (such as *student* and *faculty*) relate to other important concepts within a university environment. This model will be used to drive a single view of *person* information within the data warehouse.
- A model for a global manufacturing company showing a single way of visualizing manufacturing lot information. This model was used to level set senior managers to help them "talk the same talk."
- A model for a small health insurance company that needs to understand the big picture—that is, to understand how key concepts relate to each other. The goal is to position the organization for evaluating third-party software.

The BSAM is the most frequently built type of subject area model. Many times when we say we are creating a subject area model, we mean the BSAM. It is the most common. Before embarking on any large development effort, we first need to understand the business. If an organization needs a new claims-processing system, it needs to have a common understanding of claims and related subject areas. The BSAM can be created simply to understand a business area, or as a beginning to a large development effort, such as introducing third-party software into your organization.

Fig. 7.2 shows a BSAM for our example with the business card.

Fig. 7.2 Business card BSAM

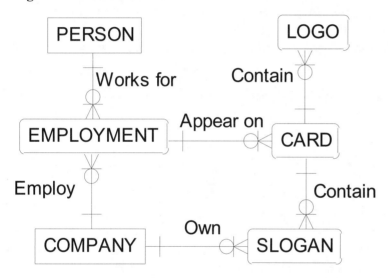

The relationships on a BSAM capture the high-level rules behind the working of a business. Not an application, but the *business*. Take a minute to read the relationships on the model, including the cardinality and labels. Make sure your reading of each relationship resembles the following sentence forms of each of the relationships:

- Each *person* can work for zero, one or many *companies*, and each *company* can employ zero, one or many *people*.
- Each *company* can own zero, one or many *slogans*, and each *slogan* must be owned by one and only one *company*.
- Each *employment* can appear on zero, one or many *cards*, and each *card* must capture one and only one *employment*.
- Each *card* can contain zero, one or many *slogans*, and each *slogan* must appear on one and only one card.
- Each *card* can contain zero, one or many *logos*, and each *logo* must appear on one and only one *card*.

When adding an associative entity such as *employment*, one of the challenges is coming up with meaningful label names from each of the two kernel entities to the associative entity. What I typically do is use the same label names that I would use on the many-to-many relationship. That is, when I read the labels, I pretend the associative entity does not exist. So rather than think of a meaningful relationship name from *person* to *employment*, I choose to add a label that describes the full relationship from *person* to *company*.

Card is a good example of the importance of the definitions of a subject area. *Card*'s definition needs to explain that this is the paper representation of a contact and not the overall subject of a business card. *Card* is a compilation of employment and formatting information such as logos and slogans. It is the grouping of information, and not the information itself, that is spread over the rest of the entities on the model. This is an important distinction, as there are times when entities can appear that really are compilations of information stored elsewhere and not the information itself. Examples of such entities are *resume*, *profit and loss report*, and *application.*

Exercise 7.2

Write a clear, complete, and accurate definition of at least one of the subject areas in fig. 7.2. (If you want a real challenge, choose the entity *person*.)

You might wonder, "Why didn't we show relationships connecting *person* to *card*, and *company* to *card*? After all, the *card* will contain information on people and the company." The answer is that we don't show derived relationships on a subject area model. If we know the *employment* information for a *card*, we automatically can derive the *person* and *company* information as well, because *employment* contains foreign keys back to *person* and *company*. If I know a particular employment instance, I know the person and company information behind the employment instance.

Also note, the layout of a data model is extremely important to its readability and therefore directly affects its communication ability. In fig. 7.2, care was taken to parallel the content of the business card with the actual presentation of the business card. I arranged the model so that the contact content appears on the left and the presentation of that content on the business card (as well as logos and slogans) appears on the right.

Exercise 7.3

Change the model in fig. 7.2 to accommodate the following business rule:

A *card* can contain information just for a *person* or just for a *company*. That is, it is not always imperative that we have a *person* and a *company*. For example, we could have Bob's Plumbing Company appear on a business card without having a person's name appear along with it.

See www.stevehoberman.com for my thoughts!

Application subject area model (ASAM)

The ASAM is a subject area model of a defined portion of a particular application. Many BSAMs are the first step in large development efforts (first understand the business before you understand the application), and therefore the BSAM is usually the starting point for the ASAM. It is also usually a subset of the BSAM subject area model. As an example, after creating the BSAM of the human resources department, we can now scope out of this an ASAM for an application tracking employee promotions.

We build two types of applications, and therefore two types of ASAMs: operational and reporting. Operational systems create data and reporting systems manipulate data to help people make effective business decisions. Operational applications maintain the health of an organization by performing daily operations, such as order processing, student registration, and the handling of insurance claims. Reporting systems turn data into information and present it in such a way that knowledge workers can make informed decisions. Business intelligence, data warehousing, decision support, and scorecards fall under the category of reporting systems.

Here are some examples of operational ASAMs building on the BSAMs mentioned earlier:
- A model for a large university showing how *person* is viewed within its student registration system
- A model for a global manufacturing company showing how manufacturing lot information is stored within SAP/R3
- A model for a small health insurance company that needs to understand how Medicare is represented in the files that the insurance company receives periodically

Here are some examples of reporting ASAMs building on the BSAMs mentioned earlier:

- A model for a large university showing how *person* is viewed within its data warehouse.
- A model for a global manufacturing company showing the sales to customers by month and manufacturing lot information.

- A model for a small health insurance company that needs to report on the claims filed per month per local region.

In our example with the business card, let's assume that we need to build two applications. The first application is a contact-management operational application and the second is a reporting application on the size of logos. The contact-management application would require the content piece of our BSAM, as all we would need to know would be *person*, *company*, and the relationship they share through *employment*. A logo-reporting application would require only the *logo* entity. See fig. 7.3 for the two ASAMs within the scope of the BSAM that we created earlier.

Fig. 7.3 Business card ASAMs

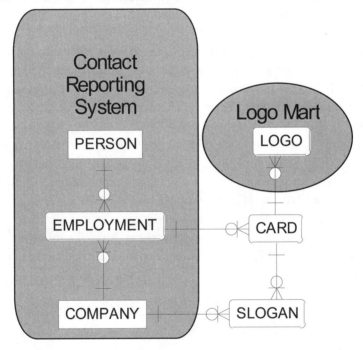

In this example, which shows only a handful of subject areas, it may be difficult to visualize the value of scoping an ASAM on a BSAM. But picture 50 to 200 or more subject areas on a BSAM. In these situations, the scoping activity can be extremely useful.

<u>Exercise 7.4</u>

What disadvantages (if any) are there with building an ASAM without first building a BSAM?

See www.stevehoberman.com for my thoughts!

Comparison subject area model (CSAM)

The CSAM is a subject area model that shows how something new fits within an existing framework. It is used primarily for impact analysis and issue resolution. CSAMs build on two or more ASAMs, in which one or more ASAMs represent an existing application environment and (optionally) one or more ASAMs represent proposed changes to an environment.

The CSAM requires the most effort to build, but of the three types of subject area models it can provide the most benefits. It requires the most effort because there is more than one viewpoint to represent on a model. Usually more than one viewpoint leads to more than one interpretation of a subject area or rules. It takes time to identify these differences and resolve, or, at a minimum, document them. The CSAM provides the most benefits because we are showing impact or issues at a high-level of granularity. What's more, it is likely that this high-level, cross-application view has not been captured and explained with such clarity previously.

Here are some examples of CSAMs, building on the operational and reporting ASAMs mentioned earlier:

- A model for a large university showing how *person* and related information are sourced from every application on campus. Strategic source systems are color-coded for ease of visualizing. These strategic sources will become the sources for their data warehouse.
- A model of a manufacturing data warehouse with a new sales-reporting application superimposed on it to show which subject areas already exist in the data warehouse and which are new. Red is used for those subject areas required by the new reporting application that are not currently residing in the data warehouse. The red subject areas will require the most effort to develop.
- A model for a small health insurance company that needs to understand the data quality issues associated with redundant claim data. Their model contains a consolidation of all the ASAMs that are considered the source for claim data. Red is used when more than one application sources the same information (in other words, where we believe there are questions about the quality of the data).

The CSAM model has two goals:

- **Identify gaps, touch points, and overlaps.** The CSAM compares something new with something in place to see whether there are gaps or redundancies. I've used a CSAM to highlight a serious customer issue we would have by bringing in a new reporting application within our existing data warehouse architecture. I've also used a CSAM to identify the strategic system sources for each subject area as pre-work to building a data warehouse.

54

- **Help estimate the development effort.** Because we are showing the overlap and gaps that a new application will cause within our environment, we can more easily develop a high-level estimate for the development effort. For example, superimposing a new reporting application over an existing data warehouse environment can help us find areas of the reporting application where the extraction, transformation, and loading (ETL) of the data will require more effort than in those areas already in the warehouse.

Let's assume that our logo data mart will be built within an existing data warehouse. We can use colors to highlight which subject areas already exist in our data warehouse and therefore require less effort and attention. For example, green subject areas are used when the subject area already exists within our data warehouse, and red subject areas are used when the subject area does not exist within our warehouse. There are a number of very useful visualization techniques, such as use of color or formatting, to make the CSAM an effective communication tool.

I'll conclude this section by showing an actual CSAM I developed several months back. See fig. 7.4. This was a CSAM showing how one company is currently using a packaged piece of software. The shaded regions represent features the packaged software provides that this organization was not yet leveraging to its fullest. I'm not going to walk through this model, because the content is not relevant to most readers. I will say, though, that this model helped clear up much confusion in this area for both business and IT team members.

Fig. 7.4 Actual CSAM example

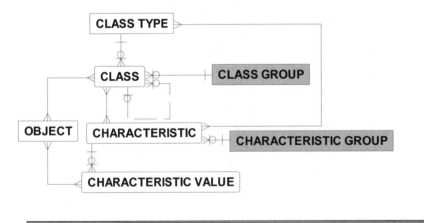

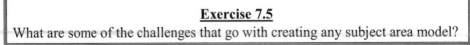

<u>**Exercise 7.5**</u>
What are some of the challenges that go with creating any subject area model?

CHAPTER 8: What is the logical data model?

A logical data model is a representation of the rules that govern the way in which something works. For example, a logical data model of insurance claims would capture the data elements that are mandatory on an insurance claim and the data rules on who can file claims (for example, a policyholder can file zero, one, or many claims).

A logical data model is at a much more granular level than the subject area model, as it contains all the data elements within our scope in a form independent of context. Context includes the things in our environment, such as database software, reporting tools, and the manner in which the data elements will be accessed within a specific application. In our example with the business card, we can capture that a *person* employed for a given *company* has at least one *phone number*. This relationship will be the same regardless of the type of application being built or the software being used.

The logical data model is constructed by applying two techniques: normalization and abstraction.

Normalization

When I turned 12, I received a trunk full of baseball cards as a birthday present from my parents. I was delighted, not just because there may have been a Hank Aaron or Pete Rose buried somewhere in that trunk, but because I loved to organize the cards. I categorized each card according to year and team. Organizing the cards in this way gave me a deep understanding of the players and their teams. To this day, I can answer many baseball card trivia questions.

Normalization is a process of applying rules to render simple and stable something that is complex. I was normalizing the baseball cards according to year and team. We can normalize the data elements within our organizations, with a different set of rules yet with the same goal of simplifying and stabilizing something complex. Just as those baseball cards lay unsorted within that trunk, our companies have huge numbers of data elements spread throughout departments and applications. We need to make things simpler and in the process gain valuable knowledge about how the business works.

The rules applied to normalizing the baseball cards entailed first sorting by year, and then by team within a year. The rules for normalizing our data elements can be boiled down to sorting them according to their correct primary and foreign keys. The end result is a simple and stable view of how a business area or application works, or should work.

In analyzing the data elements for the correct primary and foreign keys, we are forced to understand the rules governing the way a business works. We analyze each data element in order to understand not only what it is, but also how it relates to every other data element in our model. By asking questions and finding answers, we develop a strong understanding of the content of the model.

To identify the correct primary and foreign keys, we need to apply a series of more granular rules. The rules are grouped into levels according to their specificity. Each level is considered a separate normal form, starting with first normal form, which is the least specific, and concluding with fifth normal form, the most specific.

The full set of normalization levels is the following:
- first normal form (1NF)
- second normal form (2NF)
- third normal form (3NF)
- Boyce/Codd normal form (BCNF)
- fourth normal form (4NF)
- fifth normal form (5NF)

If a model is in 5NF, it is also in 4NF, BCNF, and so on. That is, the higher levels of normalization subsume the lower rules. In this text, we will be describing 1NF, 2NF, and 3NF only. 1NF ensures each entity has a valid primary key, 2NF ensures each entity has the minimal primary key, and 3NF ensures there are no hidden primary keys.

The term *normalized model* is usually interpreted to mean 3NF. BCNF, 4NF, and 5NF describe specific modeling situations that occur rarely and are therefore left to the bigger texts, such as my book, *The Data Modeler's Workbench*.

Normalization forces us to understand the content of what is being modeled. We learn how each data element relates to every other data element. Before normalization, we may have a fairly good understanding of a particular data element (such as its definition and domain), but we mostly likely lack knowledge about the way in which this data element relates to every other data element in the model. In our example with the business card, we may have identified all the data elements required for a mailing address. What is lacking, and what normalization addresses, is the way in which these address data elements relate to each other. For example, if we know a certain zip code, are we guaranteed to identify a single state and a single city?

Besides the business benefit of increased understanding, there are also several benefits to the resulting application:
- **Greater application stability.** Normalization leads to a model that mimics the way in which the business works. As the business goes about its daily operations, the application receives data according to the rules that govern the business. The model underlying the application has been structured with the knowledge that these rules can govern, and therefore the system runs smoothly as long as the rules in the business match the rules documented throughout the normalization process. If, for exam-

ple, more than one person can own an account, the model—and, therefore, the application—will accommodate this fact.

- **Faster inserts and updates.** Each level of normalization removes a certain kind of *data redundancy* from the model. Data redundancy occurs when the same information appears more than once in the same model. As redundancy is removed, changing the data becomes a quicker process, because there is less of it to update or insert. If *person's last name* appears four times on a model and Mary's last name changes, the application would have to ensure that all four occurrences of Mary's last name get updated correctly. This process is more time-consuming than a process in which Mary's last name appears only once and therefore requires only one update. Note that as redundancy is removed and change efficiency is improved, the process of retrieving data can become less efficient. If *person's last name* appears four times, the application can select the "closest" *person's last name* instance to reduce retrieval time. (There will be more on improving retrieval time when we discuss denormalization.)

- **Better data quality.** By reducing redundancy and by enforcing data rules through relationships, the data are less likely to get out of synch or violate business rules. If *person's last name* does appear four times on a model and a customer's last name changes, we need to update the last name in all four places to maintain a correct view of the information. If the application updates only three of the four instances of Mary's last name, there is a strong possibility that we will have a data quality issue. Normalization would ensure that *person's last name* existed only once on the model. The likelihood, therefore, would be lesser that a problem with data quality would arise. Normalization also leads to the portrayal of as many business rules as possible through relationships. A considerable amount of rules, therefore, are enforced on the model. If an account must have at least one account owner, the model will prevent accounts with invalid or missing account owners from occurring.

- **Faster building of new models.** Normalization ensures correct primary and foreign keys. As a result, data elements are assigned to their most appropriate entity. All data elements that require *account identifier* for uniqueness appear in *account*. All the data elements that require *slogan code* for uniqueness appear in *slogan*. There is a degree of common sense applied to the place in which data elements reside, and therefore it becomes easier to identify and re-use normalized structures on a new model. The result is more consistency across models and less time developing applications.

Starting with chaos

We have all put together puzzles at one time or another. After we open the box and dump out the pieces, the sight can be overwhelming: hundreds, maybe even thousands, of tiny pieces in a large pile. The pile is in a state of chaos. As we pick each piece up and examine it, we understand that its characteristics make it unique. We lack knowledge at this point about how these puzzle pieces connect with each other. We begin the process of fitting the pieces together and, after much effort, we complete our masterpiece. Each puzzle piece is in its proper place.

The term *chaos* can be applied to any unorganized pile, including data elements. We may have a strong understanding of each of the data elements, such as their name and definition. We lack knowledge about how the data elements fit together. We understand each piece of the puzzle, but we do not yet understand the connections between the pieces. In our example with the business card, how do the data elements *address* and *telephone number* connect? Just as we need to determine the appropriate place for each piece within our puzzle, we need to determine the appropriate place for each data element within our model.

In our example with the business card, chaos can start off as one pile of data elements. In other words, all the data elements can be initially assigned to one entity, *business card*. See fig. 8.1.

Fig. 8.1 Initial pile of data elements

BUSINESS CARD

Name
Title
Company
Email Address
Web Address
Mailing Address
Phone Number
Logo
Slogan

A good step before we tackle 1NF is to ask ourselves what makes an instance of *business card* unique. That is, what should the primary key be for *business card*?

I have found that examining actual data values from each data element usually helps answer many of the questions that arise during the normalization process. Let us, therefore, take all the values from our four business cards listed in fig. 1.1 and list them by data element. See table 8.1. We will refer to table 8.1 throughout this section.

Table 8.1 Four sample business cards in spreadsheet format.

	Name	Title	Company	e-mail address	Web address	Mailing address	Phone number	Logo	Slogan
Business card 1	Steve Hoberman	President	Steve Hoberman & Associates, LLC	me@stevehoberman.com	www.Stevehoberman.com	10 Main St New York, NY 10021	212-555-1212	Entity Model.jpg	
Business card 2	Steve Jenn		findsonline.com		findsonline.com		973-555-1212		Internet auction experts Web marketing Digital photography We'll get you the most for your item!
Business card 3	Bill Smith		The Amazing Rolando				732-555-1212		Magic for all occasions Walk around magic Children's parties Full stage shows Adult occasions Live animals & more Corporate affairs
Business card 4	Jon Smith John Doe		Raritan River Club			58 Church Avenue New Brunswick, NJ 08901	(908)333-1212 (908)555-1212 554-1212		Fine fresh seafood

When looking through this data, let's initially assume that the data elements *name*, *company*, and *phone number* are the minimal set that guarantee a unique business card instance. *Name*, *company*, and *phone number*, therefore, make up our initial composite primary key. (Note that this is not a correct assumption, but we will let normalization detect and correct this for us.) Fig. 8.2 has been updated with the addition of this primary key. Notice that the primary key always appears above the line, meaning above the horizontal line that divides the rectangle.

Fig. 8.2 Initial primary key assigned

BUSINESS CARD

Name
Company
Phone Number

Title
Email Address
Web Address
Mailing Address
Logo
Slogan

Another step worth taking before we apply 1NF is to make sure that all many-to-many relationships are resolved. Wherever there are many-to-many relationships on our model, we need to replace them with associative entities. As mentioned earlier, associative entities are dependent entities that at a minimum contain the data element foreign keys from the two entities that participate in the many-to-many relationship. Here is an example of a many-to-many relationship: each *customer* can own many *accounts*, and each *account* can be owned by many *customers*. We would need to replace this many-to-many relationship with an associative entity, such as *account ownership*. There are no many-to-many relationships in fig. 8.2, so let's move on to 1NF.

First normal form (1NF)

1NF states that every non-key data element must depend on its primary key. Another way of looking at 1NF is that for a given primary-key value, we can identify at most one of every data element that depends on that primary key. If a *customer identifier* value of 123 brings back both Smith and Jones as *customer last name* values, we have not identified the correct primary key.

Most of the time, two activities will ensure that a valid primary key is assigned to each entity:
- Move repeating data elements to a new entity.
- Separate *multivalued* data elements.

REPEATING DATA ELEMENTS

A repeating data element occurs when two or more of the same data element exist within the same entity. Repeating data elements is bad, because data elements fix the number of values an entity instance can have. If a data element is repeated three times in an entity, we can have at most three occurrences of this data element for a given entity instance. We cannot have four and we waste space if we have only one or two. Therefore, we need to move the data element that is repeating to a new entity.

Repeating data elements usually take a sequence number as part of their name. See fig. 8.3.

Fig. 8.3 Example of repeating data elements

CUSTOMER

| Customer Identifier |
| Address Line 1 Text |
| Address Line 2 Text |
| Address Line 3 Text |
| Lots of other data elements |

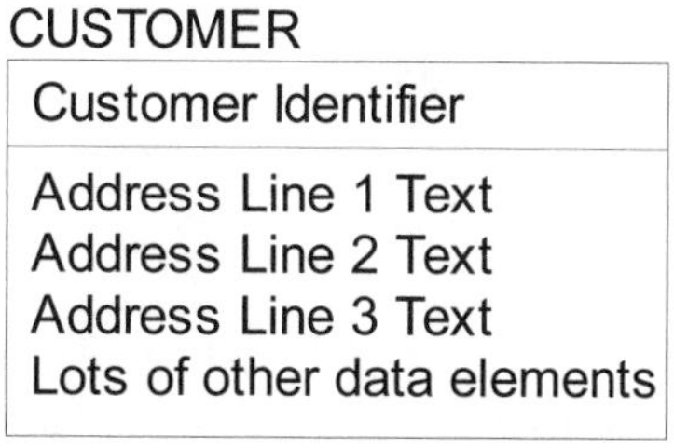

Refer to table 8.2 for some sample rows from this entity.

Table 8.2 Sample rows for *customer*

Customer Identifier	Address Line 1 Text	Address Line 2 Text	Address Line 3 Text
1	10 Main St.	New York, NY 10021	
2	PO Box 160	50 Fox Run Road	Flushing, NY 11367
3	20 Hill Road	Apartment 2B	Mount Olive, NJ 07828
4	10 Main St.	New York, NY 10021	

This is called a *repeating group*, because each address line data element is really the same data element. Each is defined as a component of the address. The components are combined to create the complete mailing address.

Now, if "Address Line 1 Text" always meant the street address, "Address Line 2 Text" always meant the post office box, apartment number, and so on, and if "Address Line 3 Text" always meant the city, state, and zip code, this would not be a repeating group. This is because each data element means something different. We would have to rename each of these data elements with more meaningful names ("Address Line 1 Text," for instance, could be renamed "Street Address Text").

Assuming these are repeating data elements, we need to create a new entity, called *address*, that has a one-to-many relationship to *customer*. See fig. 8.4.

62

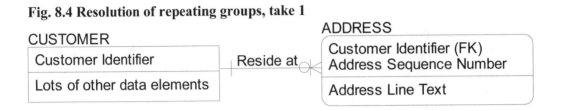

Fig. 8.4 Resolution of repeating groups, take 1

The "Address Line Text" data element is contained within *address*. The *address* composite primary key is *customer identifier* and *address sequence number*. This sequence number will indicate whether this line is the first or the fourth of the address. "Address Line Text" will contain the actual address information for this line.

Refer to table 8.3 for some sample rows from this new entity, using the same examples from table 8.2.

Table 8.3 Sample rows for *address*

Customer Identifier	Address Sequence Number	Address Line Text
1	1	10 Main St.
1	2	New York, NY 10021
2	1	PO Box 160
2	2	50 Fox Run Road
2	3	Flushing, NY 11367
3	1	20 Hill Road
3	2	Apartment 2B
3	3	Mount Olive, NJ 07828
4	1	10 Main St.
4	2	New York, NY 10021

Also notice that in creating this new entity, we have increased our flexibility. We are not constrained to three lines of address information. We can represent four, five, or 50 lines of address information for a single customer. In creating a new entity in which the primary key is the key of the original entity, we are not necessarily reducing redundancy. We are, however, increasing flexibility. We are introducing new entity instances instead of additional data elements, yet there is still the same amount of redundancy. For example, customer 1 and customer 4 live at the same address. With the model in fig. 8.4, we are repeating their complete address twice.

If a business rule existed that allowed more than one customer to reside at a single address, we would resolve this repeating group, as shown in fig. 8.5.

Fig. 8.5 Resolution of repeating groups, take 2

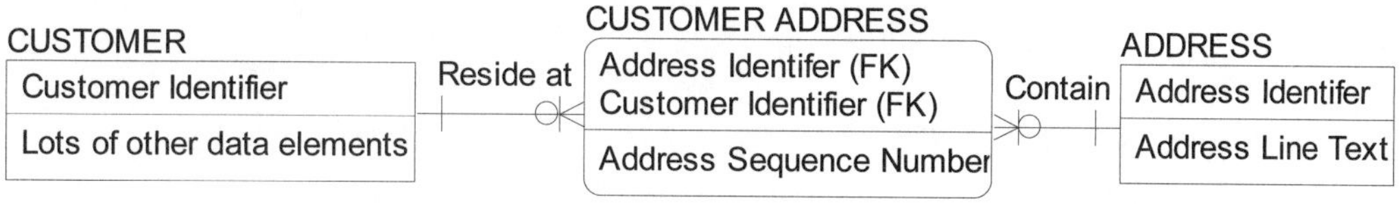

CUSTOMER — Reside at — CUSTOMER ADDRESS — Contain — ADDRESS

CUSTOMER	CUSTOMER ADDRESS	ADDRESS
Customer Identifier	Address Identifer (FK)	Address Identifer
Lots of other data elements	Customer Identifier (FK)	Address Line Text
	Address Sequence Number	

This figure shows the model allowing *address* to be shared by more than one *customer*. In this situation, each address is listed only once, and *customer address* contains the pointers between each customer and his or her address. In other words, we are treating the relationship between *customer* and *address* as a many-to-many instead of a one-to-many relationship. There is less redundancy in fig. 8.5 than in 8.4, as now the same *address* can be shared by several *customers*. Notice also we moved address sequence number to *customer address* and replaced it with a unique identifier for each address, address identifier. In so doing, we can still sequence address lines for each *customer*. Refer to tables 8.4 and 8.5 for what the same sample data would look like in each of the entities.

Table 8.4 Sample rows for *address*

Address Identifier	Address Line Text
1	10 Main St.
2	New York, NY 10021
3	PO Box 160
4	50 Fox Run Road
5	Flushing, NY 11367
6	20 Hill Road
7	Apartment 2B
8	Mount Olive, NJ 07828

Table 8.5 Sample rows for *customer address*

Customer Identifier	Address Identifier	Address Sequence Number
1	1	1
1	2	2
2	3	1
2	4	2
2	5	3
3	6	1
3	7	2
3	8	3
4	1	1
4	2	2

Exercise 8.1

Do we really need "Address Sequence Number" in *customer address* or could we use "Address Identifier" to sequence the address lines instead?

See www.stevehoberman.com for my thoughts!

There are a number of repeating data elements in our example with the business card that can be identified easily from the sample data in table 8.1. Let's look at each of these violations and refer to fig. 8.6 to see the result of making these changes.

- *Name.* This data element is repeating because we have both "Steve" and "Jenn" appearing on business card 2 and "Jon Smith" and "John Doe" appearing on business card 4.
- *Slogan.* This data element can be repeated any number of times. It occurs seven times on business card 3.
- *Phone Number.* At first, this data element appears to be a repeating group, as we can see more than one phone number for the fourth business card and can imagine in most cases that there could be more than one phone number on a business card. However, is this really a repeating group? That is, is it really the same data element appearing more than once in the same entity? No. All these phone numbers may share the same phone number domain, but each has a different role. We cannot consider this a repeating data element. One is a main number, another a fax number, another a mobile number, and so on. If we determine that there is no meaning assigned to a phone number being listed first, second, or third, we can deduce that

phone number has the same definition for each occurrence and therefore this can now be considered a repeating group.

Fig. 8.6 Business card model with repeating groups resolved

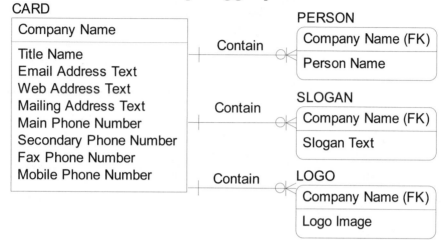

When referring to fig. 8.6, you will notice that *logo* was treated as a repeating group as well, even though on our representative set of four business cards there was at most only one logo on a card. At times, our common sense about the way the world works combined with validating this common sense with the business leads to additional changes to the model. Similarly, asking questions to the business, such as "Do you need other types of phone numbers?" have also led to the creation of *mobile phone number*, which did not appear on any of the four cards.

You may have noticed that in many cases the data element names in fig. 8.6 have been expanded with the addition of a suffix. This is called a *class word*. A class word represents the high-level domain of a data element. It is shown as the last term in a data element's name. Examples of class words are *code*, *name*, *date*, *quantity*, *identifier*, and *amount*. It is a good modeling practice to end each data element with a class word, as it decreases the opportunity for more than one piece of information to be stored within the same data element and increases the clarity of the model. For example, there is a greater chance that there will be more confusion in understanding the contents of *gross sales* than *gross sales amount*. The name *gross sales amount* also reveals that a financial amount is stored in this data element, instead of a weight, volume, or quantity. For a complete list of class words as well as a resource for naming structure and syntax in general, refer to the ISO Information Technology 11179 standard.

MULTIVALUED DATA ELEMENTS

Multivalued means that within the same data element we are storing at least two distinct values. In other words, we need to ensure that each data element is atomic and contains only one value. For example, *name* may contain both a first name and last name. *First name* and *last name* can be considered distinct data elements, and therefore "John Smith" stored within *name* is multivalued, because it contains "John" and "Smith."

There are also a number of multivalued data elements, which are shown resolved on the completed 1NF model in fig. 8.7:

- *Person's name.* This data element contains all the portions of a person's name, which could be any of a combination of *last name*, *first name*, *middle name*, *name prefix* (such as "Dr."), *name suffix* (such as "Jr."), and so on. For this example, we will keep it simple and just break out *name* into *first name* and *last name*. Note that it is easier to model the components of *name* than to implement a parsing algorithm to extract a single *name* field into all its components. This is one of the reasons why I prefer the modeling side!

- *E-mail and Web address.* Both of these data elements contain all the components of an internet address (e.g., domain). Would it be wise to break these data elements up into their pieces? Yes, if we are designing a domain registry or similar application. However, if we are designing a contact-management database, the business most likely views e-mail address and Web address as atomic data elements themselves, and therefore we do not need to break these down further.

- *Phone number.* This data element contains the area code and several other pieces of information. For simplicity in our example, let's treat the phone numbers as atomic, but realize if this was an application related to telecommunications or marketing, we would most likely break down *phone number* into its components.

- *Mailing address.* This data element is crammed with other data elements, such as *street address*, *city*, *state*, and *zip*. I have seen models in which the street address itself was broken down into smaller pieces, such as whether the street is an avenue, road, place, and so on. Realize as the analyst that we need to determine whether this level of detail would be valuable. Also, we need to decide on the scope of the address set. That is, can we have addresses outside the country? If we can, that changes not only the set of data elements we will need (we will need a *country code*, for example), but also the names and domains for each of the data elements. *Zip code* will need to be globalized into *postal code*, for example. To illustrate 1NF in our modeling example, let's assume the scope is limited to the United States and break out the main components of address: *street address*, *city*, *state*, and *zip code*.

Exercise 8.3

Assume that there is a need to represent a global address structure. Create a logical data model of a complete global-address structure. Note: you may need to go through 2NF and 3NF before completing your model.

See www.stevehoberman.com for my thoughts!

Let's end this discussion of multivalued data elements with a practical note. A modeler will encounter multivalued data elements that in many cases do not need to be separated into distinct data elements. This is common when the business or industry views the data element as atomic, even though it contains more than one piece of information. Among the examples that we have encountered in this section are *e-mail address* and *phone number*.

The cost of unnecessarily breaking apart a multivalued data element is extra development effort to parse and then put the pieces back together for the business user, as well as jeopardizing data quality should the data element be broken up or reconstructed incorrectly. We need to be practical when deciding which data elements to parse. If there is any doubt about whether a data element should be broken into its components, I would recommend breaking it apart. It is easier to put the components back together than to come up with parsing logic after the application is in production.

Fig. 8.7 Business card model in 1NF

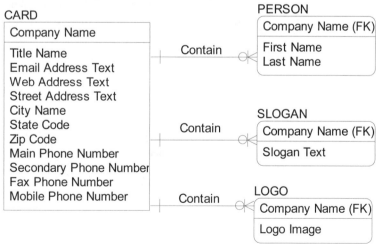

Exercise 8.4

Assume that some slogans are more important than others. For example, some of the business cards have a main slogan in the center followed by smaller and less important slogans around the corners of the cards. For example, assume that greater importance is placed on "magic for all occasions" than the other six slogans on business card 4. Adjust the model in fig. 8.7 for this change.

See www.stevehoberman.com for my thoughts!

Also, this model is still far from being completely normalized. We can look at some of the primary and foreign keys and realize they are not correct. For example, *company name* does not uniquely identify a *person*, and a *person* can own many *cards*, not just one, as the current model states. If we don't get the primary key correct in 1NF, then we will definitely get it correct in 2NF, as we will see in the next section.

Second normal form (2NF)

Our completely normalized model will have the correct set of primary and foreign keys, with each level of normalization adding rules to help us get closer to this goal. 2NF contributes to this goal by requiring each entity to have the minimal correct primary key—in other words, a minimal set of data elements to uniquely identify each entity instance.

In more formal terms, 2NF states that we must remove non-key data elements not dependent on the whole primary key. As we noted earlier, non-key data elements are all data elements except for primary, foreign, and alternate keys. A data element that depends on only part of the primary key is called a partial key dependency. We want to make sure our primary keys are correct, and we want to remove any partial key dependencies.

For example, in fig. 8.8 we have *employee assignment*.

Fig. 8.8 Example of model not in 2NF

EMPLOYEE ASSIGNMENT

| Employee Identifier |
Department Identifier
Employee Last Name
Department Name
Department Cost Center

The primary key to *employee assignment* is *employee identifier* and *department identifier*. Do we have the minimal primary key for each of the non-key data elements? No. *Employee last name* needs only *employee identifier* to uniquely identify one of its values. Similarly, both *department name* and *department cost center* need only *department identifier* to uniquely identify its values. Therefore, we need to modify this model to get it into 2NF, as shown in fig. 8.9.

Fig. 8.9 Example of model now in 2NF

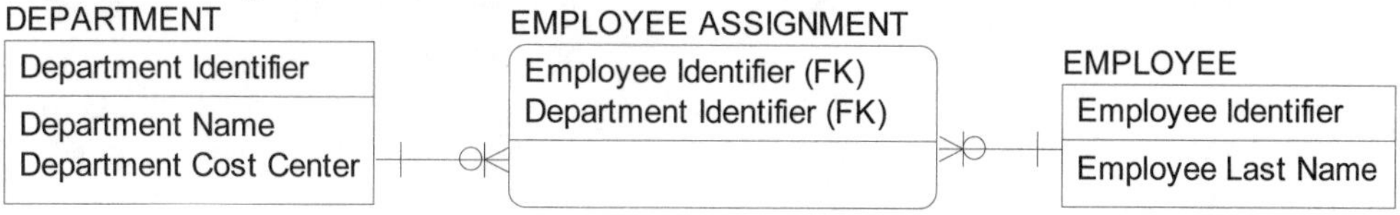

DEPARTMENT

Department Identifier
Department Name
Department Cost Center

EMPLOYEE ASSIGNMENT

Employee Identifier (FK)
Department Identifier (FK)

EMPLOYEE

Employee Identifier
Employee Last Name

Now *department name* and *department cost center* depend only on *department identifier*, and *employee last name* depends only on *employee identifier*. The associative entity *employee assignment* links employees with their departments.

The completed 2NF model for our example with the business card is shown in fig. 8.10. After applying the 1NF rules, we realize that all the current primary keys need work. The culprit appears to be *card*, which contains data elements that belong to other entities. As an aside, entities that represent reports, forms, or other types of documents usually contain many data elements that need to be moved into other entities to satisfy 2NF.

We need to create a *company* entity which contains only those data elements dependent on a company and not on the card that a company owns. The same is true for the contact information that appears on the card. This contact information is specific for a *person* who works for a given *company*, and is therefore also not dependent on the card. As in our *employee assignment* entity in fig. 8.8, we need to create an associative entity between *person* and *company* called *employment*.

70

Fig. 8.10 Business card model in 2NF

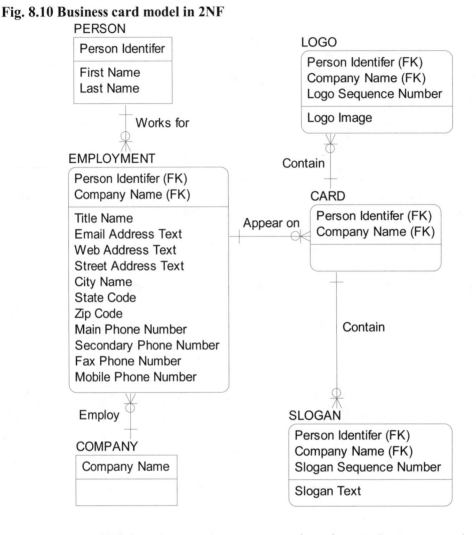

In this example, 2NF forced us to separate content from format. Content comprises the information that could appear on a business card, and format includes how this information (along with other formatting elements such as logo and slogan) is represented on the business card. Content is *person*, *employment*, and *company*. Format is *logo*, *card*, and *slogan*.

Here are the changes made to our 1NF model for 2NF:

- ***First name* and *last name* depend on *person*, not *card*.** I created the surrogate key *person identifier* as the primary key for *person*. As mentioned earlier and as will be discussed in detail under physical data modeling, surrogate keys are integer counters that substitute for the real primary key of an entity. You will notice a number of surrogate keys added to this model. Wherever we use surrogates, we should strive to find an alternate key. In this example, I did not add an alternate key, because *person first name* and *person last name* are not unique. That is, there can be two or more people with the name John Doe.

Exercise 8.5

Is there anything available on a business card that could be used as an alternate key for *person*? If not, what would make an ideal alternate key for a *person*?

See www.stevehoberman.com for my thoughts!

- Company name depends on company, not card.
- *Contact information* depends on the relationship between a *person* and *company*. *Employment* contains title, addresses, and phone numbers. We are making the assumption that title, addresses, and phone numbers do not belong to a person or the company he or she works for but rather to the relationship between a person and a company. Bob, for example, will have a different phone number when he works for company ABC than when he works for company XYZ.
- *Card* can contain many *logos* and *slogans*. Sequence numbers are added to the *logo* and *slogan* primary keys to allow for multiple values on the same card and also the name "sequence" implies that this data element can be used for prioritizing the values on a card. For example, in table 8.6 are the values that might exist in *slogan* for business card 3.

Table 8.6 Sample rows for *slogan*

Person Identifier	Company Name	Slogan Sequence Number	Slogan Text
3	The Amazing Rolando	1	Magic for all occasions
3	The Amazing Rolando	2	Walk around magic
3	The Amazing Rolando	3	Children's parties
3	The Amazing Rolando	4	Full stage shows
3	The Amazing Rolando	5	Adult occasions
3	The Amazing Rolando	6	Live animals & more
3	The Amazing Rolando	7	Corporate affairs

Third normal form (3NF)

Even though there are higher levels of normalization than 3NF, many interpret the term "normalized" to mean 3NF. This is because the higher levels of normalization (that is, BCNF, 4NF, and 5NF) cover specific situations that occur much less frequently than the first three levels.

3NF requires the removal of hidden dependencies. Each non-key data element must be directly dependent on the primary key, and not directly dependent on any other non-key data elements within the same entity. Let's look at the model in fig. 8.11. In this example, *employee age count* and *employee gender text* are 3NF violations.

Fig. 8.11 Example of model not in 3NF

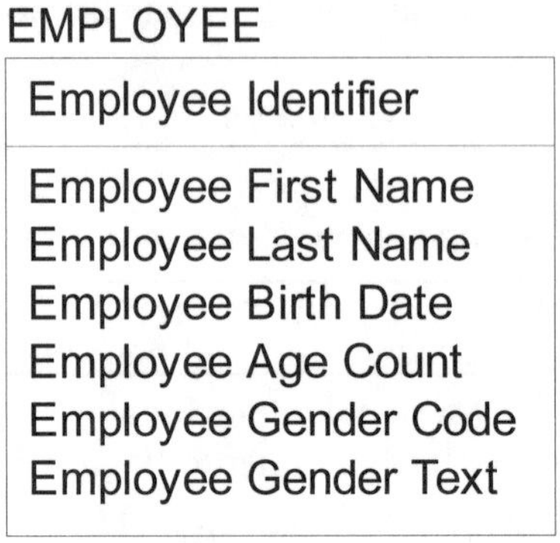

EMPLOYEE

Employee Identifier
Employee First Name Employee Last Name Employee Birth Date Employee Age Count Employee Gender Code Employee Gender Text

Employee age count is a derived data element. Derived data are built from other data. For example, a numeric calculation such as *gross sales amount* is derived by multiplying *list price* by *order quantity*. A descriptive data element such as *order late indicator* is a yes/no field that says whether an order was delivered late. It is derived by examining *requested delivery date* and *actual delivery date*. In this case *employee age count* is calculated from *employee birth date* and today's date. Derived data is a 3NF violation, because the derived data element depends on those data elements from which it is derived and not directly on the primary key.

Employee gender text depends not on employee identifier but on employee gender code. See table 8.7 for sample data showing employee identifier, employee gender code, and employee gender text. "Male" and "female" depend directly on the employee gender code.

Table 8.7 Sample rows for *employee*

Employee Identifier	Employee Gender Code	Employee Gender Text
3	M	Male
4	F	Female
123	F	Female
57	M	Male
8	M	Male

To make the model in fig. 8.11, 3NF requires removing the derived data element and creating a separate lookup table for gender, as shown in fig. 8.12.

Fig. 8.12 Example of model now in 3NF

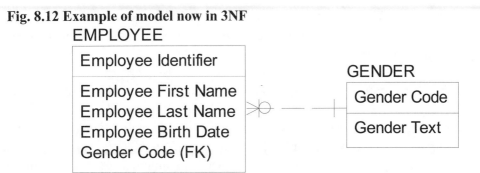

Note that by naming the entity *gender* instead of *employee gender*, we can use this lookup table for other people entities, such as *customer* and *supplier*.

3NF violations almost always fall into the two categories illustrated in this example:
* derived data
* decodes embedded with codes in non-lookup entities

By looking at our 2NF business card data model from fig. 8.10, we can see *zip code* depends on the *city* and *state*, and therefore *city* and *state* do not depend directly on *employment*. This is shown resolved in fig. 8.13:

Fig. 8.13 Business card model in 3NF

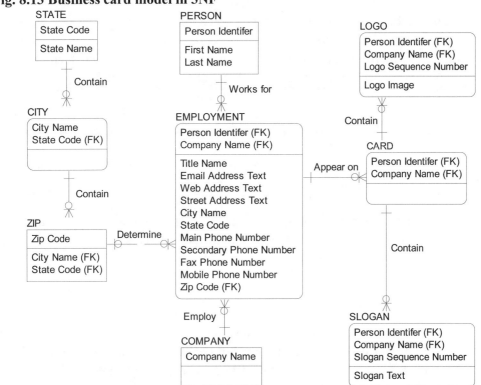

Notice that the relationship between *state* and *city* is identifying, because *city name* is not unique across states. There is a city called Oceanside in New York and a city called Oceanside in California, for example.

You will find that the more you normalize, the more you go from applying rules sequentially to applying them in parallel. For example, instead of first applying 1NF to your model everywhere, and then when you are done applying 2NF and so on, you will find yourself looking to apply all levels at once. This can be done by looking at each entity and making sure the primary key is correct and that it contains a minimal set of data elements, and that all data elements depend directly on the primary key.

A final note on normalization. Normalization has its roots in mathematics. Each level of normalization is defined within the guidelines of relational set theory. Texts focusing on the set-theory side of normalization emphasize that the by-product of normalization is a structure that prevents update anomalies and data inconsistencies through the removal of redundancy. This is definitely true, but at times even more valuable is the increased understanding of how the business works through normalization. Therefore normalization should be defined in simple terms so that it is easily understood and used often, as we have done in this section. We trade formalization for simplicity.

Exercise 8.6

Practice normalizing using a document you come into contact with outside work. It could be a menu in a restaurant, a prescription-drug bottle, or any application form you find yourself filling out. Imagine that all the labels on the document are instances of data elements and produce an optimal normalized design.

Abstraction

For artists, abstraction is a tool. It lets them efficiently capture and represent complex topics. We data modelers are artists to an extent, and abstraction is an efficient tool at our disposal also.

The data modeler is responsible not only for correctly representing the requirements of an application, but also for having the foresight to design flexible structures in areas where requirements may change in the near future.

Abstraction is part of the logical data modeling process and is usually performed after normalizing. Abstraction brings flexibility to your logical data models by redefining and combining some of the data elements, entities, and relationships within the model into more generic terms. Abstraction is the removal of details in such a way as to broaden applicability to a wide class of situations while preserving the important properties and essential nature from concepts or subjects. By removing these details, we remove differences and therefore change the way we view these concepts or subjects, including seeing similarities that were not apparent or even existent before.

For example, instead of having separate *customer* and *employee* entities, there may be situations in which it would be valuable to have the generic *person* entity. *Person* can include concepts that may need to be added to an application in the near future. If *contractor* is required by an application that is built upon a model that already uses *person*, many (or even all) of the data elements and relationships assigned to *person* might also be applicable for *contractor*, and therefore the model and application will experience few or no changes.

Abstraction can also reduce analysis and design time if we choose to abstract before (or instead of) normalizing. If we lack time or knowledgeable subject-matter resources (people and documentation), we can abstract instead of normalize. We will not need to perform a thorough analysis of the requirements, and this saves substantial time. For example, if we are not sure what types of people will exist within our application, adding *person* allows us to accommodate any type of person.

Within two weeks, I was able to create a model showing the entire manufacturing industry through frequent abstraction. Instead of spending considerable amounts of time analyzing each data element, I abstracted to make sure any possible requirement was handled within the model. I knew that the manufacturing industry embraces a wide range of transactions, such as shipments, debits, and credits. Rather than spend time modeling each transaction and risk getting the model incomplete or incorrect, I added *transaction* to my model. It is important to realize that you might save time here, but you can also forfeit an understanding of the business requirements that comes with normalization. If you have the time, normalize first and then abstract.

In our example with the business card, we have several types of phone numbers in *employment*: main phone number, secondary phone number, fax phone number, and mobile phone number. "Types" is the keyword behind abstraction, as if you abstract you tend to only model the "types" and therefore your model can accommodate other types of phone numbers without modification. Fig. 8.14 contains an abstraction of *phone number*.

Fig. 8.14 Business card model with abstraction

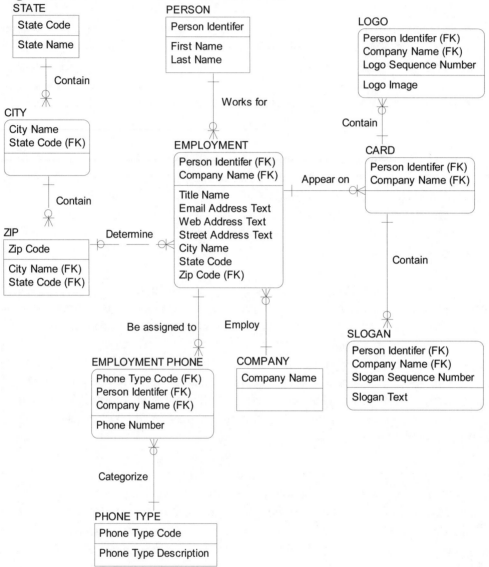

Table 8.8 contains *employment* instances from our 3NF model from fig. 8.13. Only the relevant data elements are shown. I added the person's name in parenthesis after the *person identifier* to make it easy to trace back to the actual business cards from table 8.1.

Table 8.8 Instances of *employment* before abstraction

Person Identifier	Company Name	Main	Secondary	Fax
1 (Steve Hoberman)	Steve Hoberman & Associates, LLC	212-555-1212		
2 (Steve)	findsonline.com	973-555-1212		
3 (Jenn)	findsonline.com	973-555-1212		
4 (Bill Smith)	The Amazing Rolando	732-555-1212		
5 (Jon Smith)	Raritan River Club	(908)333-1212	(908)555-1212	554-1212
6 (John Doe)	Raritan River Club	(908)333-1212	(908)555-1212	554-1212

To illustrate how these values are stored after abstraction, refer to table 8.9, which contains the instances from *employment phone* in fig. 8.14.

Table 8.9 Instances of *employment phone* after abstraction

Phone Type Code	Person Identifier	Company Name	Phone Number
Main	1 (Steve Hoberman)	Steve Hoberman & Associates, LLC	212-555-1212
Main	2 (Steve)	findsonline.com	973-555-1212
Main	3 (Jenn)	findsonline.com	973-555-1212
Main	4 (Bill Smith)	The Amazing Rolando	732-555-1212
Main	5 (Jon Smith)	Raritan River Club	(908)333-1212
Main	6 (John Doe)	Raritan River Club	(908)333-1212
Secondary	5 (Jon Smith)	Raritan River Club	(908)555-1212
Secondary	6 (John Doe)	Raritan River Club	(908)555-1212
Fax	5 (Jon Smith)	Raritan River Club	554-1212
Fax	6 (John Doe)	Raritan River Club	554-1212

Notice the extra flexibility we gain with abstraction. A new phone number for find-sonline.com, for example, leads to a new row instead of a new data element on a model with subsequent application changes. Abstraction allows for greater flexibility but does come with a price, actually three high prices: loss of communication, loss of business rules, and longer development time.

When we abstract, we lose the actual business data element name. We convert column names to row values. For example, we can't find *fax phone number* on the model in fig. 8.14. One of the main reasons we model is for communication, and abstracting can definitely hinder communication. Some modelers list some of the sample values of the abstract structure as text near the abstract entity. So for example, next to *phone type* could appear "main, secondary, fax, mobile." Reducing communication is a by-product.

There is also a loss of business rules on an abstract model. In the unabstracted model in fig. 8.13, for example, it is easy to enforce that every *employment* instance have a *main phone number*. However, there is no longer a way to do this in the model in fig. 8.14, as *main phone number* is now a row and not a data element. The more we abstract, the fewer rules we can show and enforce on the model.

Although we can decrease analysis and design time using abstraction, we most likely increase development time. It takes longer to write code and logic against row values than against data elements. For example, it is not a trivial task to write the code to populate or select information out of *employment phone*. To experience this, look at the model in fig. 8.13 and walk through the logic required to display all the phone numbers for an *employment* instance. However, if the data source for the abstract structures is also stored in a similar abstract format, the development effort will be minimized.

Also, there are some reporting tools on the market today that have a very difficult if not impossible time extracting data from abstract structures. There have been several cases in which I introduced abstraction into the physical data models only to reverse this decision because the reporting tool, and the query language in general, had difficulty retrieving information from these structures.

An important tip to ensure that the reader applies abstraction only where worth doing so is to apply the rule of two. If you have identified at least two "types" of similar things on your model, is there a chance that there could be a third or fourth type of this same thing? For example, if you've identified both a home and work address in *person*, could *person* have other types of addresses as well? If the answer is yes, then abstract address.

Exercise 8.7

Abstract all other areas you think would add value in fig. 8.14.

See www.stevehoberman.com for my thoughts!

Exercise 8.8

Identify at least one abstract structure currently part of an application in your organization. Would you consider it a successful use of abstraction?

Identify at least one structure currently part of an application in your organization that should have been abstracted but was not. What have been the costs of not abstracting this structure?

Exercise 8.9

Abstract the following data model:

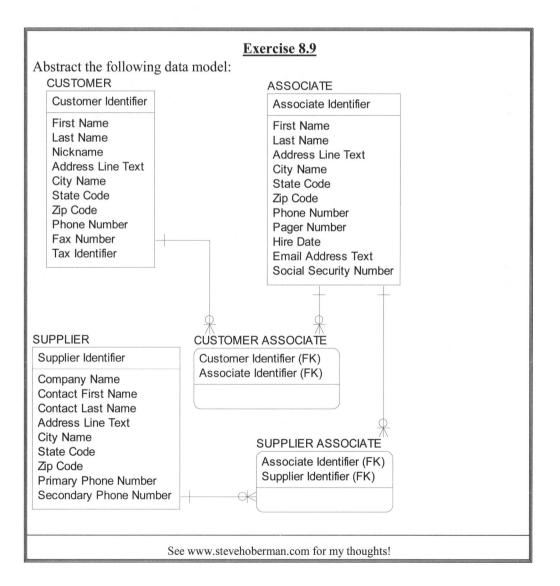

See www.stevehoberman.com for my thoughts!

CHAPTER 9: What is the physical data model?

The logical data model represents the rules behind how the business or application works independent of context. The physical data model represents the rules behind how the business or application is optimized for a specific context. Context includes two categories: tools and usage.

Tools include all the software and hardware and networking components of the application. Physical data models based upon the same logical data model will vary greatly if one is for an application to be run on Microsoft Access and another is for an application to be run on Teradata, for example. A physical data model designed for Microsoft Access will vary quite a bit from its logical data model to compensate for the lack of scalability and robustness present in Access. Teradata, however, is a much more powerful platform. As a result, a physical data model designed for Teradata will more closely resemble the logical.

Usage includes how the actual data is going to be manipulated by the users of the system. Both a sales-reporting system and order-entry system will have almost identical logical data models, because the content of these two systems is almost identical. However, their physical models will be very different, because they have different usages. The sales-reporting system will be used solely for data retrieval and therefore its physical data model needs to be optimized for query. The order-entry system will be used mostly for entering data and therefore its physical data model needs to be optimized for inserting and changing data.

We turn our logical data model into a physical data model that works well in a given context by using a number of modeling techniques, including denormalization, surrogate keys, indexing, partitioning, views, and dimensionality. We'll discuss each of these in this section, with extra emphasis placed on denormalization, as this is the most common of the physical modeling techniques.

Denormalization

Denormalization is the process of selectively violating normalization rules and reintroducing redundancy into the model. This extra redundancy can reduce data retrieval time, which is the primary reason for denormalizing. We also can denormalize to create a more user-friendly model. For example, we might decide to denormalize company information into an entity containing employee information, because when employee information is retrieved, company information is usually also retrieved.

The faster retrieval and user-friendliness, however, come with the price of extra redundancy on the model, which could in turn

- **Cause update, delete, and insert performance to suffer.** When we repeat the value of a data element, we can usually reduce retrieval time. However, if we have to change the value that we are repeating, we need to change it wherever it occurs. If we are repeating *company* information for each *employee*, for example, and a *company name* value is changed, we will need to make this update for each *employee* instance that works for this company.

- **Take up more space.** In a table with a small number of records, extra storage space incurred by denormalization is usually not substantial. However, in tables with millions of rows, every character could require megabytes of additional space. You might be thinking that space is cheap. It is true that space is becoming cheaper every day. However, I recently had to purchase more storage space for one of my projects, and I was amazed at the amount of time required to go through the budgeting process and red tape to actually receive the storage space. Space was cheap, but time was not.

- **Introduce data quality problems.** By having the same value appear multiple times, we substantially increase opportunities for data quality issues when those values change. Imagine, for example, if we failed to update all *employee* instances of a company name change if company information is denormalized into *employee*. Also, denormalizing reduces the number of relationships and therefore reduces the amount of referential integrity on our model. Denormalizing company information into *employee* means we can no longer enforce the rule that each *employee* must work for a valid company.

- **Stunt growth of the application.** When we denormalize, it can become harder to enhance structures to meet new requirements, because before we add data elements or relationships we need to understand all the hidden rules on the physical data model that were shown on the logical data model. If *year* and *month* are denormalized into *day*, we can quickly retrieve year and month information when viewing a particular day. However, it would be very challenging to expand this denormalized time structure to add *week*, for example. We would have to sort through all the redundant data and then add new redundant data for *week*.

There are five denormalization techniques:

- standard
- repeating groups
- repeating data elements
- FUBES
- summarization

We will apply each of these five techniques to *logo* and *card* from our logical data model. The relevant subset of our logical data model appears in fig. 9.1.

Fig. 9.1 Subset of business card logical data model

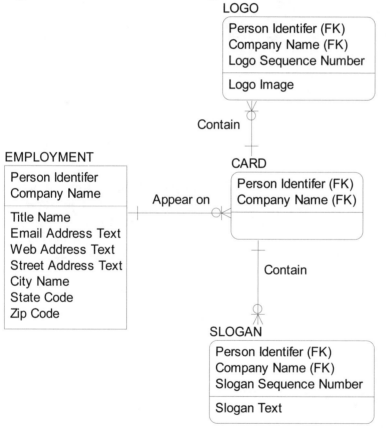

STANDARD

The standard method is the most common of the five denormalization techniques. The parent entity in the relationship disappears, and all the parent's data elements and relationships are moved to the child entity. Recall the child entity is on the many side of the relationship and contains the foreign key back to the parent entity, which appears on the one side of the relationship. Fig. 9.2 shows the standard way of denormalizing, using *card* and *slogan* as an example.

84

Fig. 9.2 Example of standard technique

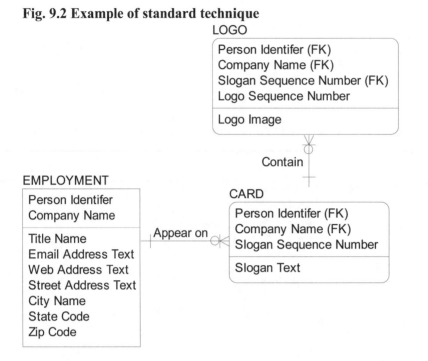

Even though we retained the name *card* in fig. 9.2, it is really no longer *card* but instead *slogan*. The primary key of *card* is equivalent to *slogan*'s primary key and *slogan text* now appears in *card*. I chose to name the denormalized entity "*card*" because it made the most sense in this situation. A majority of the time, however, we tend to keep the name of the child entity, as this is the level of granularity we now have when applying the standard technique.

Relationships where the parent entity was dependent on another entity fold together without introducing additional foreign keys. It follows the formula: If A then B, if B then C, therefore if A then C. *Card* was dependent on *employment*, so the *employment* primary key appeared on *card* as a foreign key. *Slogan* was dependent on *card*, and therefore the *card* primary key appeared on *slogan* as a foreign key. When *card* was denormalized into *slogan*, the relationship to *employment* was moved to *slogan*. As a result, there are no additional foreign keys, as the foreign key was already in *slogan* through the relationship to *card*.

Relationships where the parent entity was a also a parent to other entities now have the child entity's primary key appearing everywhere the parent entity's primary was appearing before being denormalized. This is shown in the relationship that used to exist between *logo* and *card* and now exists from *card* and *slogan* combined to *logo*. Notice that we now have a *slogan sequence number* appearing in the primary key of *logo*, which does not make business sense.

Also, what if we have a *card* that has no slogans? If we decide to use this physical data model in our application, we tend to let the data enforce the business rule instead of the previous relationships. What this means is that we do something "creative" such as having the first value in *slogan* have a value of 1, knowing there is a possibility of having no value in *slogan text*. See table 9.1 for an example of two cards represented through the now de-normalized *card*.

Table 9.1 Sample instances of *card*

Person Identifier	Company Name	Slogan Sequence Number	Slogan Text
1	Steve Hoberman & Associates, LLC	1	Not applicable
4	The Amazing Rolando	1	Magic for all occasions
4	The Amazing Rolando	2	Walk around magic
4	The Amazing Rolando	3	Children's parties
4	The Amazing Rolando	4	Full stage shows
4	The Amazing Rolando	5	Adult occasions
4	The Amazing Rolando	6	Live animals & more
4	The Amazing Rolando	7	Corporate affairs

Exercise 9.1

What issues can occur by allowing a Slogan Sequence Number of 1 to indicate "Not Applicable"?

See www.stevehoberman.com for my thoughts!

The standard way of denormalizing should be chosen in the following situations:

- **When you need to maintain the flexibility that existed on the normalized model.** So each *card* contained zero, one or many *slogans* on our logical, and we want to preserve this flexibility in our physical.
- **When a majority of the time the retrieval required is only at the lowest level.** That is, retrieval is at the *slogan* level and there is seldom a need for *card* level data elements and relationships.
- **When a user-friendly structure is required.** At least one relationship has been removed making it less complicated for users to navigate (assuming users have access to the underlying structures which is a large assumption).

REPEATING GROUPS

In the repeating-groups technique, the same data element or group of data elements is repeated two or more times in the same entity. Also known as an *array*, a repeating group requires fixing the number of times something can occur. Recall that in 1NF we removed repeating groups and here it is being reintroduced. An example of a repeating group appears in fig. 9.3.

Fig. 9.3 *Employee* with repeating group

EMPLOYEE

Employee Identifier
Address Line Text 1
City Name 1
State Code 1
Zip Code 1
Address Line Text 2
City Name 2
State Code 2
Zip Code 2

On our logical data model, each *employee* can reside at zero, one, or many addresses. On our physical data model, we have fixed the number of addresses an *employee* can reside at to at most two.

Repeating groups have many uses. A common use is to represent a report that needs to be displayed in a spreadsheet format. For example, if a user is expecting to see a sales report in which sales is reported by month for the last 12 months, an example of a repeating group containing this information is shown in fig. 9.4.

Fig. 9.4 Sales-report entity with repeating group

SALES SUMMARY REPORT

Product Identifier Month Code Year Code
Current Month - 1 Total Sales Amount Current Month - 2 Total Sales Amount Current Month - 3 Total Sales Amount Current Month - 4 Total Sales Amount Current Month - 5 Total Sales Amount Current Month - 6 Total Sales Amount Current Month - 7 Total Sales Amount Current Month - 8 Total Sales Amount Current Month - 9 Total Sales Amount Current Month - 10 Total Sales Amount Current Month - 11 Total Sales Amount Current Month - 12 Total Sales Amount Lots of other sales report data elements

At the end of a given month, the oldest value is removed and a new value is added. This is called a *rolling 12 months*. Faster performance and a more user-friendly structure lead us to adding repeating groups in this example and purposely violating 1NF.

See fig. 9.5 for an example of a repeating group using a subset of our business card model.

Fig. 9.5 Example of repeating-group technique

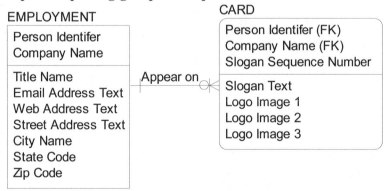

The *logo* child entity gets used often with *card* information and therefore it makes sense to store the data together. However, *card* is one of the central concepts on our model and therefore needs to be preserved. After careful analysis, we believe (and more importantly, the business believes) that we never can have more than three logos on a given business card. Therefore we fold up the child entity *logo* into the parent entity *card*.

The repeating-group technique should be chosen in the following situations:

- **When it makes more sense to keep the parent entity instead of the child entity.** It can make more sense when the parent entity is going to be used more frequently than the child or if there are rules and data elements useful to preserve in the parent entity format.
- **When an entity instance will never exceed the fixed number of data elements added.** We know we will never have more than three logos on a card, for example. 'Never' is a strong word though and if we ever had four logos it would require structural changes to our model and resulting application or loss of data.
- **When you need a spreadsheet.** As seen in fig. 9.4, repeating groups work well if there is a need to view a report in a spreadsheet format. We would repeat the one or more data elements that appear in the spreadsheet column headers. This can lead to producing the report in less time than by stringing together a large number of entity instances.

Repeating groups, however, are extremely limited for any other purpose other than for primarily spreadsheet type reporting. If we would like to know in fig. 9.5 for example how many logos are in gif format versus how many logos are in jpg format, we need to search across all three data elements. "Is Logo Image 1 .jpg or .gif? What about Logo Image 2? Now let's do Logo Image 3." This is similar to the limitations we would face by trying to use the sales-reporting structure in fig. 9.4 to do quarterly sales reporting. Imagine the difficult in trying to determine which months roll up to which quarters and then summing the amounts.

Due to repeating groups being extremely useful for a very particular need, I recommend storing the repeating group in at least one other format to accommodate additional needs that might arise. For example, in fig. 9.4, it might make sense to also store this information in a more normalized structure such as what appears in fig. 9.6.

Fig. 9.6 This entity should accompany the entity in fig. 9.4

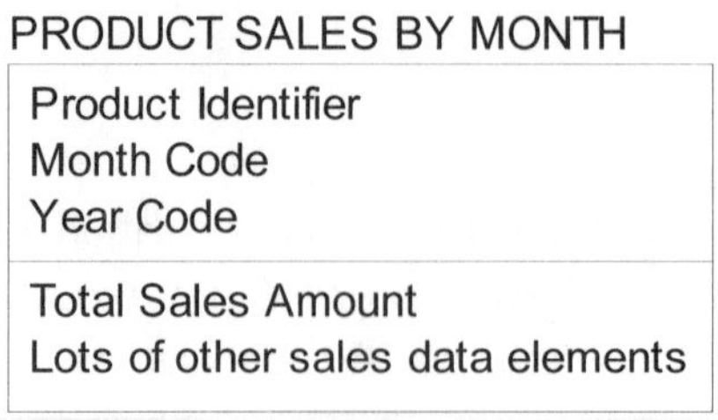

PRODUCT SALES BY MONTH

| Product Identifier |
| Month Code |
Year Code
Total Sales Amount
Lots of other sales data elements

Exercise 9.2

Fig. 9.4 shows sales over the last 12 months. Assume there is a reporting need to see sales over the last 24 months, not for the last 12 months. Would you prefer to continue to use the model in fig. 9.4, or repeat a set of data elements for 24 months as shown in the following entity? Explain your answer.

SALES SUMMARY REPORT

Product Identifier
Month Code
Year Code

Current Month - 1 Total Sales Amount
Current Month - 2 Total Sales Amount
Current Month - 3 Total Sales Amount
Current Month - 4 Total Sales Amount
Current Month - 5 Total Sales Amount
Current Month - 6 Total Sales Amount
Current Month - 7 Total Sales Amount
Current Month - 8 Total Sales Amount
Current Month - 9 Total Sales Amount
Current Month - 10 Total Sales Amount
Current Month - 11 Total Sales Amount
Current Month - 12 Total Sales Amount
Current Month - 13 Total Sales Amount
Current Month - 14 Total Sales Amount
Current Month - 15 Total Sales Amount
Current Month - 16 Total Sales Amount
Current Month - 17 Total Sales Amount
Current Month - 18 Total Sales Amount
Current Month - 19 Total Sales Amount
Current Month - 20 Total Sales Amount
Current Month - 21 Total Sales Amount
Current Month - 22 Total Sales Amount
Current Month - 23 Total Sales Amount
Current Month - 24 Total Sales Amount
Lots of other sales report data elements

See www.stevehoberman.com for my thoughts!

REPEATING DATA ELEMENTS

The repeating data-elements technique is when you copy one or more data elements from one entity into one or more other entities. It is done primarily for performance because by repeating data elements across entities we can reduce the number of joins needed to return results. If we repeat *customer last name* in *order* for example, we avoid navigating back to *customer* whenever just *customer last name* is needed for display with order information.

See fig. 9.7 for an example of this technique using a subset of our business card model.

Fig. 9.7 Example of the repeating data-elements technique

EMPLOYMENT

```
┌─────────────────────────┐
│ Person Identifer        │
│ Company Name            │
├─────────────────────────┤
│ Title Name              │
│ Email Address Text      │  ── Appear on ──◁
│ Web Address Text        │
│ Street Address Text     │
│ City Name               │
│ State Code              │
│ Zip Code                │
└─────────────────────────┘
```

CARD

```
┌─────────────────────────┐
│ Person Identifer (FK)   │
│ Company Name (FK)       │
│ Slogan Sequence Number  │
├─────────────────────────┤
│ Title Name              │
│ Slogan Text             │
│ Logo Image 1            │
│ Logo Image 2            │
│ Logo Image 3            │
└─────────────────────────┘
```

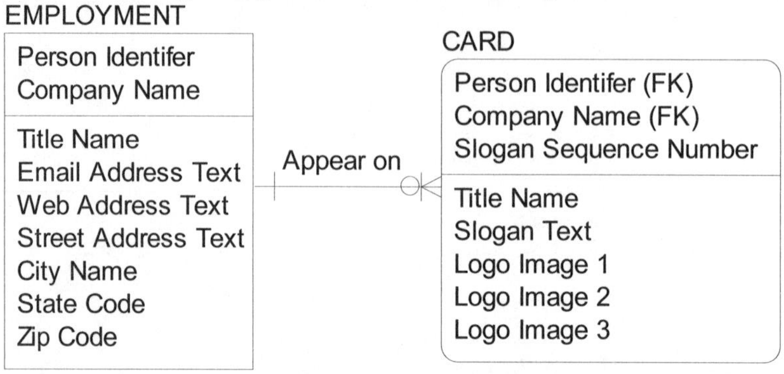

Somewhat facetious, but let's assume that job title is directly dependent on the turnaround time in printing business cards. CEOs should receive their cards quicker than data modelers, for example. By repeating *title name* in *card* we avoid having to go back to *employment*. Note if I need e-mail address text or any other *employment* data element I will need to navigate back anyway. It is only when I just need *title name* where the time savings occurs.

The repeating data elements technique should be chosen in the following situations:

- **When the repeated data element or elements are accessed often and experience little or no changes over time.** If for example, *title name* changes frequently, we would be required to update this value on *employment* and for each of the cards tied to an *employment* instance. This takes time to update and could introduce data quality issues if not all updates were performed correctly or completely.
- **When the standard denormalization option is preferred but space is an issue.** Possibly there would be too huge an impact on storage space if the entire parent entity was folded up into the child and repeated for each child value. Therefore only repeat those data elements that provide the greatest benefits.

Exercise 9.3

Which subject area do we tend to most frequently apply repeating data elements from?

See www.stevehoberman.com for my thoughts!

FUBES

FUBES (fold up but easily separate) is an acronym I made up for a technique that combines the standard method of denormalizing with also allowing access to just the parent data elements. There is an additional data element that contains a level code and additional instances for each of the parents. An example of FUBES appears in fig. 9.8.

Fig. 9.8 *Time* using FUBES

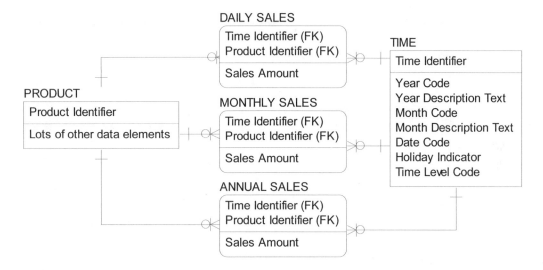

Table 9.2 Contains sample values for some of the data elements in *time*.

Table 9.2 Several instances of *time*

Time Identifier	Year Code	Month Code	Date Code	Time Level Code
1	2005			Year
2	2005	Jan		Month
3	2005	June		Month
4	2005	June	6/1/2005	Date
5	2005	June	6/2/2005	Date

Although I did not show all the time data elements, you can see that for each child we are repeating the parent level data elements, just like the standard method. In addition, the *time level code* lets us immediately access parent instances which we could not do with the standard method. *Daily sales* will have a foreign key back to *time* where the *time level code* is equal to *date*, as in *time identifiers* 4 or 5. Likewise *monthly sales* might possibly point back to *time identifiers* 2 or 3. *Annual sales* possibly to a *time identifier* of 1.

FUBES is the most flexible denormalization option, and also takes up the most space. See fig. 9.9 for an example from our business card model.

Fig. 9.9 Example of FUBES

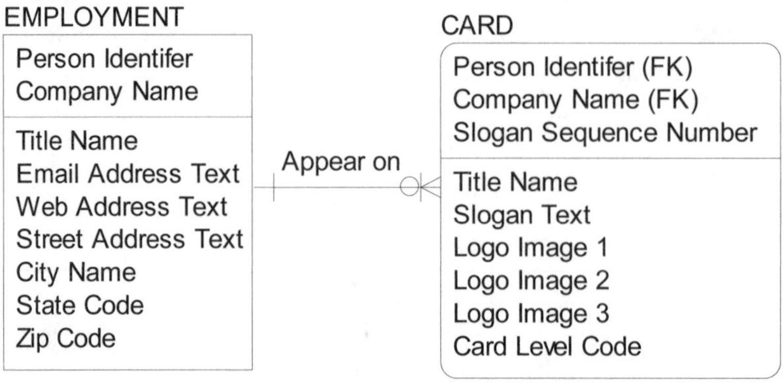

EMPLOYMENT   CARD

EMPLOYMENT	CARD
Person Identifer Company Name	Person Identifer (FK) Company Name (FK) Slogan Sequence Number
Title Name Email Address Text Web Address Text Street Address Text City Name State Code Zip Code	Title Name Slogan Text Logo Image 1 Logo Image 2 Logo Image 3 Card Level Code

Appear on

Card level code distinguishes which level we are referring to, containing either the value *card* or *slogan*. If we will be continuously accessing *card*-level data, having the *card level code* may be a good idea.

FUBES should be chosen when there is value in denormalizing yet there is a still a need to access parent instances. Having an instance for each parent allows us to achieve better report performance as we can directly tie to parent levels without having to roll up from the child. We can store sales at a year level for example and save the time of summarizing daily level sales up into a year level.

The drawback for FUBES is that you need to include the level code in all the queries on the table. So for example, to access month information, we would need to select on the primary key plus where *time level code = month*. This requires slightly more complexity in queries and can lead to errors if this data element is accidentally omitted from queries.

Exercise 9.4

Describe at least two other frequent modeling situations where having an additional data element to distinguish entity instances adds value. In other words, what other data element besides a level code would be useful for distinguishing different types of entity instances?

See www.stevehoberman.com for my thoughts!

SUMMARIZATION

Summarization is used when there is a need to report on higher levels of granularity than what is captured on the logical data model. *Daily sales*, *monthly sales*, and *annual sales* from fig. 9.8 are all summary tables derived from the actual order transactions.

Fig. 9.10 shows a summary table used to answer questions on the quantity of business cards produced for a given company.

Fig. 9.10 Example of summary table

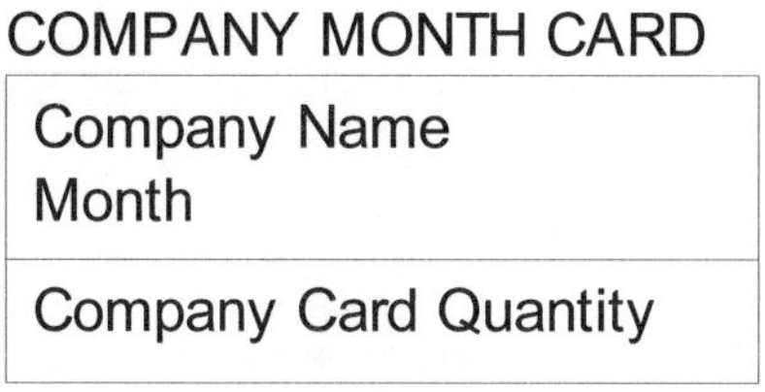

COMPANY MONTH CARD

Company Name Month
Company Card Quantity

The summary table in this example allows the user to answer high-level questions without spending time figuring out how to do it with very low-level tables, and the response time is much quicker, because of the highly summarized nature of the data.

However, summary tables come with the cost all the denormalization options come with: extra redundancy. Extra redundancy from the summary tables not only takes up more space but leads to extra development effort. It takes a greater time of the batch processing window to populate. Make sure the value is greater than the cost.

Exercise 9.5

Name at least five factors we should consider before creating a summary table.

See www.stevehoberman.com for my thoughts!

Surrogate keys

A surrogate key as was previously defined is a unique identifier for a table. Characteristics of a surrogate key include that it is an integer that has no meaning based on its value. That is, you can't look at a *month identifier* of 1 and assume that it represents the month of January. It is usually a system generated counter. Surrogate keys are in almost all cases not visible to the business staying "behind the scenes" while the business continues to see what they consider as unique for each entity.

Surrogate keys provide for a number of benefits, the two most important being facilitating integration and permitting more efficient joins across tables.

- **Integration.** Applications such as data warehouses often require data from more than one application. If the same subject area such as *customer* or *claims* exists in more than one system, there is a good chance some amount of integration will be needed. Integration is an effort to create a single and consistent version of the data. Surrogate keys can be defined across source systems, so that a Robert Jones from system XYZ and a Renee Jane from system ABC might both be identified in their respective systems as RJ, but once they are loaded into an integrated application they are each assigned a unique non-overlapping value. Similarly, if Robert Jones is identified as RJ in system XYZ and BJ in system DEF, this will need to be identified and consolidated under a single surrogate key value. Note that in all cases it is easier to model the integrated structure than it is to actually identify and consolidate the actual data from the sources.

- **Efficiency.** Also, surrogate keys are integer and therefore take up less space and provide quicker joins than other formats or composite keys. *Promotion identifier* is a more efficient primary key than a 10-character *promotion code* and date format *promotion start date*.

In our example with the business card, *person identifier* is a surrogate key. Refer to table 9.3 for several surrogate key values from *person*.

Table 9.3 *Person identifier* sample values

Person Identifier	First Name	Last Name
1	Steve	Hoberman
2	Steve	
3	Jenn	
4	Bill	Smith
5	Jon	Smith
6	John	Doe

Are Steve Hoberman and Steve really the same person? If yes, this will need to be resolved under a single *person identifier*. Note how difficult this can be to resolve without having something unique in each instance that is in common. For example having Social Security number in Steve Hoberman and Steve would be a useful data element to have in realizing these both represent the same person.

Company Name in our example with the business card is a good candidate for a surrogate key. This is because *company name* could be a fairly long text string, such as Steve Hoberman & Associates, LLC. Also, if a *company name* value ever were to change, we would be updating a primary key (and foreign keys back to this primary key), which is a practice we want to avoid. If we were to create a *company identifier* primary surrogate key, it would be a good idea to create an alternate key on *company name*.

I strongly recommend creating an alternate key on an entity when using a surrogate key as a primary key. This is because the alternate key is really what is unique about the entity, and will be used by developers to distinguish updates from inserts, and by the business in retrieving instances.

There might be times however, when it is not possible to assign an alternate key when using a surrogate key. If there is truly no way to uniquely identify an entity instance, then we can't use the term *surrogate key*. This is because a surrogate key is a substitute for the actual key, and if we don't have an actual key then we don't have a surrogate key. We use the term *virtual key* in this situation. A virtual key is used when there is no unique way to identify an entity instance. In the manufacturing environment for example, there is a transaction generated whenever a case of product is move from one warehouse shelf to another. This move is important to track, yet can be impossible to identify. If we create an *assignment identifier* as the primary key for the entity containing these transactions, then *assignment identifier* would be considered a virtual key.

Exercise 9.6

What is a good format and length for a surrogate key?

See www.stevehoberman.com for my thoughts!

Exercise 9.7

Identify at least one situation in which it does not make sense to use a surrogate key.

See www.stevehoberman.com for my thoughts!

Indexing

An index is a pointer to something that needs to be retrieved. An analogy often used is the card catalog, which in the library points you to the book you need. The card catalog will point you to the place where the actual book is on the shelf, a process that is much quicker than looking through each book in the library until you find the one you need. Indexing works the same way with data. The index points to the place on the disk where the data is stored, reducing retrieval time.

Indexes work best on data elements that are being retrieved and very rarely updated. Indexes also provide the most value as you might expect for tables with many rows, like *customer* and *order*, or on data elements in smaller tables that join to large tables. Indexing is very specific to the underlying database and you might find what works well on one database platform falls short on another.

Primary keys, foreign keys, and alternate keys are automatically indexed just by the fact that they are keys. A non-unique index, also known as a secondary key, is when an index is added to one or more non-key data elements. *Card level code* would make a great secondary key, because it is a data element that will be queried on often.

Partitioning

Partitioning is breaking up a table into rows, columns or both. If a table is broken up into columns, the partitioning is vertical. If a table is broken into rows, the partitioning is horizontal.

Fig. 9.11 contains an example of both horizontal and vertical partitioning.

Fig. 9.11 Example of horizontal and vertical partitioning

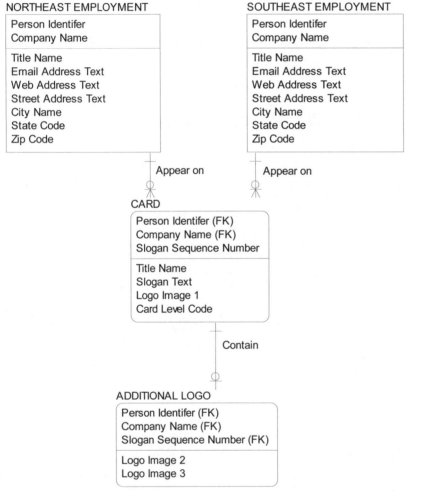

Employment has been horizontally partitioned by geography. Those *employment* instances whose addresses reside in the Northeast are kept in *Northeast employment* and those in the Southeast are kept in *Southeast employment*. A popular reason for horizontal partitioning is for security so those users can only see the records that are pertinent to their region.

Logo Image 2 and Logo Image 3 have been vertically partitioned into *additional logo*. We now have a one-to-one relationship between *card* and *additional logo*. Vertical partitioning is also done often for security reasons, but in this particular example it could be done more for space reasons if we determine that a very high majority of the time there is at most one logo on a card.

Views

A view is a virtual table. It is a "view" into one or many tables or other views that contain or reference the actual data elements. I like to think of a view as a hybrid of a table and query, as views are nothing more than queries that resemble tables.

We abstracted phone number in our example with the business card earlier in the text, which leads to greater flexibility but is more difficult to extract the actual phone information. In fig. 9.12 we created a view to "unabstract" the main phone number, which is needed quite often by business users.

Fig. 9.12 Example of view

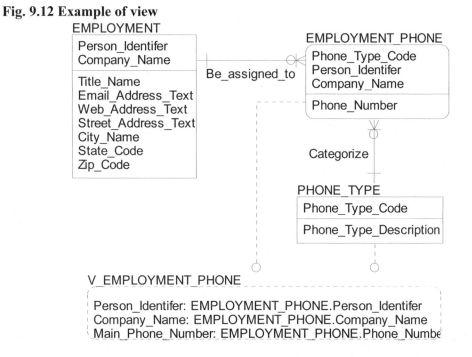

A view is shown on the model as a rectangle with rounded corners and outlined by a dotted line. There is SQL query language behind the view. This query joins these two tables on Phone_Type_Code and then selects those phone numbers where the Phone_Type_Description equals *main*. I could have also found out the Phone_Type_Code for *main* and join on that value directly, but to illustrate a bit more complex SQL, I chose the description. I also could have retrieved *first name* and *last name* for a given *person identifier*, but that would complicate the view without adding value to this example.

Here is what the SQL looks like behind the view V_EMPLOYMENT_PHONE:

```
CREATE VIEW V_EMPLOYMENT_PHONE
(Person_Identifer, Company_Name, Main_Phone_Number)  AS
    SELECT EMPLOYMENT_PHONE.Person_Identifer,
EMPLOYMENT_PHONE.Company_Name, EMPLOYMENT_PHONE.Phone_Number
    FROM EMPLOYMENT_PHONE, PHONE_TYPE
    WHERE EMPLOYMENT_PHONE.Phone_Type_Code =
PHONE_TYPE.Phone_Type_Code
AND PHONE_TYPE.Phone_Type_Description = 'Main'
```

There are different types of views, with the standard view invoking the SQL to retrieve data at the point when a data element in the view is requested. It can take quite a bit of time to retrieve data depending on the complexity of the SQL and the data volume. However there are types of views such as materialized views or snapshots that can match and even sometimes beat retrieval speed from actual tables because they are generated at some pre-determined time and stored in system cache.

Views are a popular choice to assist with security and user-friendliness. If there are sensitive data elements within *employee* such as *employee salary information*, then a view can select only those non-sensitive data elements from *employee*. Views can also take some of the complexities out of joining tables for the user or reporting tool.

In fact, we can use views in almost all situations where we are using denormalization. Views can offer at times all the same benefits as denormalization *without the drawbacks associated with data redundancy and loss of referential integrity*. A view can provide user-friendly structures over a normalized structure, thereby preserving flexibility and referential integrity. A view will keep the underlying normalized model in tact and at the same time present a denormalized or summarized view of the world to the business.

There are two factors that can lead the modeler to choose denormalization over views. Both factors have to do with time:

- **History.** If there is a derived data element that needs to remain constant over time for example, storing it as a data element in a denormalized table would allow capturing the "as occurred" value whereas storing in a view would only present the most current calculation of the information. For example, a salesperson's commission at the time a sale is made should be calculated and stored to prevent seeing the current result if calculated in a view (unless a current result is what is required).
- **Currency.** In terms of currency, we need to decide if the view can provide timely data to meets the requirements. For example, if there is a need to show an end of day snapshot of all the orders for a given product, a standard view would most likely not be acceptable because it would display the end of day plus any transactions up to and including when the view when accessed.

Dimensionality

The Data Warehousing Institute defines *business intelligence* (BI) as "the processes, technologies, and tools needed to turn data into information, information into knowledge, and knowledge into plans that drive profitable business action." We need to structure our data in such a way to make it as user-friendly, accessible, and intuitive as possible so that it can be used effectively to make decisions. Deciding on the right type of model for a BI application requires an understanding of the type of question decision makers need addressed.

For example, consider the following questions:

- What is my gross sales amount by region, product, and month?
- What are the names of my top 10 most profitable customers by month for the last two years?
- How many members do we have by county and state over the last five years?

Questions that return data elements that can be mathematically manipulated require a different structure than questions that return description information. Those that return descriptive information such as *customer name* in the second question are modeled using traditional relational modeling techniques.

The book *Mastering Data Warehouse Design* by Imhoff, Galemmo, and Geiger has a great definition of a relational model: "The relational model is a form of data model in which data is packaged according to business rules and data relationships, regardless of how the data will be used in processes, in as non-redundant a fashion as possible." To relate this definition to the context of this book, all the modeling techniques we spoke about so far are for the relational model. For example, we should apply normalization and abstraction to the logical relational model and selectively apply denormalization to the physical data model. Relational models are built for operational applications and for BI applications that return description information.

Data elements that can be mathematically manipulated such as summed or averaged are called *measures*. BI applications that answer business questions with measures are modeled using dimensional modeling techniques. The first and third questions return measures and fig. 9.13 contains a dimensional model of the third question, the gross sales amount question.

Fig. 9.13 Sales dimensional model

- What is my gross sales amount by region, product, and
  month?

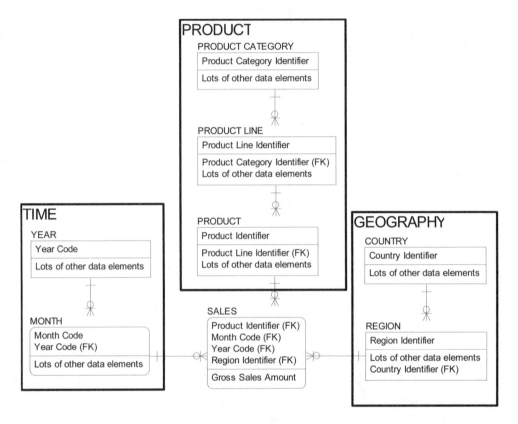

A dimensional model is a data model whose only purpose is to allow efficient and user-friendly filtering, sorting, and summing of measures. The relationships on a dimensional model represent reporting navigation paths instead of business rules as with the relational model.

The measures on a dimensional model are put in a central table called a meter. The meter in fig. 9.13 is *sales*. All the different ways of filtering, sorting, and summing measures are structured within dimensions. Dimensions are subject areas whose only purpose is to add meaning to the measures. *Gross sales amount* can be retrieved with any combination of month, product or region. The beauty of a dimensional structure is that reporting tools and knowledge workers can easily drill up to higher levels of granularity such as from *month* to *year*, or drill down to lower levels of granularity such as from *country* to *region*.

There are two major rules in a dimensional structure that make it efficient for reporting on measures:

- **All relationships from dimensions connect through the meter.** That is, you can never have relationships between different dimensions. You cannot show for example in the dimensional model from fig. 9.13 the rule capturing which products can be sold within which region, as this would require a relationship between *product* and *region*.

- **Dimensions are structured according to the reporting requirements for displaying the measures.** Entities are not formed based on the rules of normalization or denormalization, but rather by considering the ways in which the measures can be retrieved. *Gross sales amount* can be displayed at different time spectrums such as *year* and *month*, therefore each of these would be represented as distinct levels. Note that although most dimensions are hierarchies such as all the dimensions in fig. 9.13, there are exceptions such as dimensions representing simply a code and description.

Exercise 9.8

Which of the following queries require a dimensional model?

```
-   Show me the names of all alumni who have donated more
    than $50,000 over the last five years.
-   Show me our donations by class, region, and year.
-   Show me our top-selling brands by region and year.
-   Show me our gross revenue by brand by region and year.
```

See www.stevehoberman.com for my thoughts!

Refer to fig. 9.14 for our business card initial dimensional model. The word *initial* is used because this model can experience one more major design change that will be considered shortly.

Fig. 9.14 Initial dimensional model

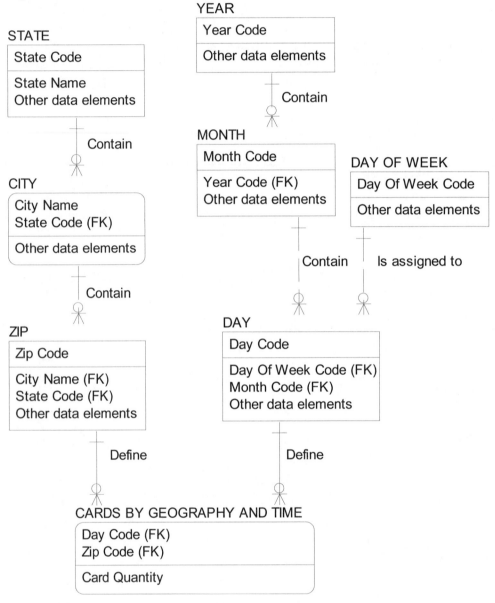

In this example the business needs to know the quantity of cards sold by geography and time. The measure *card quantity* is stored within the meter *cards by geography and time* and there is both a *time* and *geography* dimension. The dimensional model is the first step in a physical design. Changing this model further into a *star schema*, *snowflake*, or *star-flake* is the next step.

In a star schema, the tables that make up a dimension are folded into one table. The resulting table is at the level of detail of the more granular table in the hierarchy. For example, if *month* and *year* are folded together the resulting entity will be at a *month* level.

A star schema is very easy to create from the initial dimensional model and visually appears elegant and simplistic to both IT and the business. For these reasons it is often used in many situations where it is not the optimal design choice. It is most useful when the dimensions have relatively few rows and the levels within a dimension experience minimal or consistent value changes. For example, very rarely would the levels in *geography* or *time* experience value changes. Therefore, these dimensions are static and good candidates to have their levels folded up together.

Refer to fig. 9.15 for an example of a star schema for our example with the business card.

Fig. 9.15 Star Schema

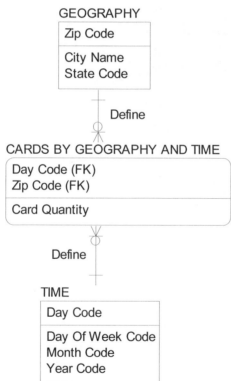

A snowflake occurs when the initial dimensional model is implemented without folding up any tables. Therefore, the snowflake design in most cases looks exactly as it does in fig. 9.14. There are many reasons for which tables are not folded up. The most common reason is that the rates at which data values change might vary across hierarchy levels.

A starflake is a combination of the snowflake and star schema. Certain dimensions have all their levels folded into a single table, whereas other dimensions have their hierarchy levels remain in separate tables. Applying guidelines when to fold up at a dimension level instead of at a model level can easily lead to a starflake as some dimensions for example experience varying rates of change such as *customer* while others remain relatively static such as *time*.

Exercise 9.9

Build an initial dimensional model for a consumer affairs department that has the following request:

```
Show me the number of complaints, compliments, and ques-
tions by product, month, and region.
```

Next, convert your model into a star schema, snowflake, or starflake, depending on what you think is most appropriate.

See www.stevehoberman.com for my thoughts!

Exercise 9.10

Do you think it is easier to create a dimensional model or a relational model? Explain your answer.

See www.stevehoberman.com for my thoughts!

CHAPTER 10: What is the best approach to building the models?

One of the questions I get asked often during our data modeling courses is, "Where do I begin?" That is, now that we understand subject area, logical, and physical data models, which of these models are required for my project, and what is the order in which they should be built? There are two equations we can apply to come up with a modeling approach:

- purpose + audience = deliverables
- deliverables + resources + time = approach

This first equation determines the "what," and the second determines calculates the "how." The "what" equation identifies the reason we are modeling and focuses on the needs of our audience. Unfortunately, all too often this first equation is seldom applied and instinctively we instead turn our attention solely to the second equation. The "how" equation calculates how we should best proceed in completing the modeling deliverables based on the real world constraints of resources and time. Success requires that both equations be applied by the project team.

Purpose + audience = deliverables

"Begin with the end in mind" is an exhortation that Stephen Covey repeats throughout his writings on time management. It is one that applies nicely to the purpose component of this equation. Why are we doing the modeling? Before we draw a single rectangle or line, we need to identify for a particular effort why we even need a data model. We need to select at least one of the reasons we mentioned earlier:

- to build a new application
- to understand an existing application
- to perform impact analysis
- to understand a business area
- to facilitate training and education

Once we identify at least one of these reasons, we next need to consider our audience. Our audience will determine the level of detail required, selecting from a combination of subject area, logical, and physical data models.

Table 10.1 shows each of the reasons we do data modeling categorized by whether the audience has a business, functional, or technical background. Most managers and business users fit into the business audience. Functional analysts, designers, and architects fit into the functional audience. Developers and testers fit into the technical audience.

Table 10.1 Which models to build

	Business	Functional	Technical
Building a new application	Subject area	Logical	Physical
Understanding an existing application	Subject area	Logical	Physical
Performing impact analysis	Subject area, Physical	Subject area, Physical	Subject area, Physical
Understanding a business area	Subject area, Logical	Subject area, Logical	Subject area, Logical
Training and education	Subject area, Logical	Subject area, Logical	Subject area, Logical, Physical

In building a new application or understanding an existing application, I have found subject area models to be very useful for not just identifying the scope of an effort, but also for building rapport with business people. Rapport building is accomplished by working together at the white board or flipchart sketching out high-level concepts and their relationships. I was once the modeler for a consumer interaction BI application which allowed users to run reports on what consumers thought of their products. The manager of the consumer interaction business area and I spent several hours sketching boxes and lines on a white board. This time spent was invaluable in the development effort that followed, and helped build a relationship of trust and understanding between IT and the business.

If the audience has a functional background, their needs for building a new application or understanding an existing application are usually identical to the business needs plus the need for more detailed understanding down to a data element level, which is where the logical data model can help. Although a business person might cringe when the word "normalization" is mentioned, it is up to the functional people to translate the business person's understanding of the data elements and rules in an application into a structure that is fully normalized. During a series of meetings where we were building a financial application for example, I played the role of the functional analyst and built the logical data models literary under my desk as I listened and asked questions to the business users walking through their processes.

If the audience has a technical background, the subject area and logical data models might be useful for understanding, but the physical data model is what they need to work from. I have found a number of technical people I have worked with to be very open and eager to learn how the business works from the subject area and logical data models. I have also experienced the opposite reaction, where due to time constraints or lack of interest, developers preferred to solely work from the physical and not spend time understanding the logical or subject area.

Impact analysis is the identification of how something new is going to impact something in place, such as replacing or enhancing applications. Subject area models work very well to show impact analysis of potentially large changes. Replacing a legacy order processing system with an ERP package or adding a new reporting application to an existing data warehouse are examples where subject area models will be effective.

You might think we should never show a physical data model to a business person, however sometimes showing a physical data model to a business person can be a very effective tool to illustrate complexity. Almost the opposite effect we would expect from data modeling. Very recently, a business person wanted to routinely achieve some of the data in one of our ERP packages. Their understanding was that it would be a very simple activity to perform and only impact five or six different tables. I built a physical model of this area and showed it to the business person to illustrate that archiving in this area is a much more complex activity and involved literary hundreds of structures that needed to be analyzed and considered for archiving.

Independent of audience, understanding a business area or educating others at a high level is best accomplished with a subject area model. Understanding a business area and training others at a data element level requires a logical data model.

If you are working with an audience crossing business, functional, or technical backgrounds, you will most likely need to produce more than one type of model. This statement might be common sense yet can be at odds with the *time* element of the next equation. We often realize that we are not given the time to build all three types of models.

Deliverables + resources + time = approach

Once we've addressed the first equation we now understand the deliverables we need to produce. To determine the approach we will take to produce these deliverables requires an awareness of available resources and time.

Resources include both people and documentation. People who understand the way the business works or who have an understanding of the application requirements. Documentation encompasses the source systems, requirements documents on the new system, reports, and so on.

Time includes how much time is available for the overall project in general and the modeling activities in particular. Unfortunately, this is the factor of the equation we at times have the least control over. I have worked on projects where the dates were set without even a high-level understanding the requirements! When dates are set according to factors outside our control, we can either attempt influencing those who set these dates if we feel they are unrealistic, or revisit the required deliverables. Usually those modeling activities that are done more for the good of the organization and not directly beneficial to the specific project are the first activities to be cut when time gets tight. Activities not directly beneficial to the project might include name standardization, definitions, and subject area and logical data modeling in general.

One of my modeling courses is a data modeling workshop where participants have to build an unrealistic number of models in a single day. Most teams under this time pressure deliver only the physical data model. After all, this is the only model that is really mandatory in building a new system. The physical data model is used to directly generate the required database tables.

So to summarize, if you are given only enough time to produce one data model and your goal is to develop database tables, you want to make sure you produce the physical data model. If, however, you have enough time to produce the one or more data models to satisfy your audience and modeling objective from table 10.1, you can build these models according to one of three approaches as shown in fig. 10.1. If you are building just two of the three models shown in fig. 10.1, you can still choose an approach. Just remove the model you are not producing from the chart. So for example, if all you need is a subject area and logical model, pretend the physical data modeling box does not exist in fig. 10.1.

Fig. 10.1 Modeling approaches

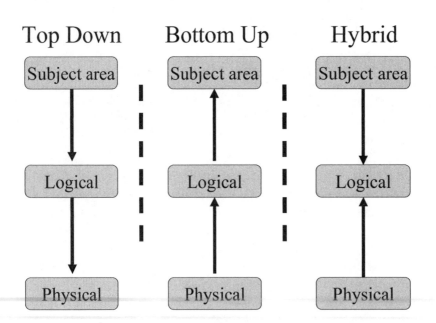

In the top-down approach, we let the requirements completely drive the modeling. We start with a subject area model that is based purely on what is needed in the resulting business area or application. The logical data model is built next showing all the rules that exist between the data element. Then the logical structure is modified to perform within a given environment in the physical data model.

This approach is ideal when there are no existing applications that need to be considered during the project. That is, there is not a need to source data from another system or send data to another system. If there is a sourcing requirement, the top-down approach usually requires a mapping effort at the physical level where data elements identified as requirements are mapped to source system data elements or downstream system data elements. More than likely in this situation, mapping gaps will be identified where requirements differ from what is available and therefore there will be an impact to the logical and subject area models.

If we consider the top-down approach to be a representative of the "dreamer" in each of us as we are driving it from what we want, then the bottom-up approach can be viewed as the "realist" in each of us. The bottom-up approach starts with an existing application and works upward toward understanding the logical and subject area views of this application. One of the industry terms for when we derive a data model from an existing database is called "reverse engineering." The bottom up technique can simply be used to understand how an application works, or can be combined with the top-down approach in an effort to first understand how the existing environment works, and then propose a future way that the business should work.

In the hybrid approach, we do both top down and bottom up and meet somewhere in the middle. One example of the hybrid approach that I use quite often is to build a subject area model of a set of requirements. Next, I assign all the data elements needed from source systems to each subject area and then normalize to create the logical data model. Afterward, I make physical changes such as denormalization and indexing to complete the physical data model.

Exercise 10.1

Which modeling approach would be ideal for gauging the impact of customizing a brand new ERP package? Explain your answer.

See www.stevehoberman.com for my thoughts!

CHAPTER 11: How do I validate a data model?

In eighth-grade social studies, the teacher gave us the assignment of writing a 100-page essay on one of the 50 states. I was assigned South Carolina. I didn't know much about South Carolina, but I learned quite a bit during the weeks I spent writing this paper. When the paper was returned to me, I was very surprised to see that I had received a failing grade. In flipping through the pages, I noticed that the only comment the teacher made in the entire paper was that he did not like my drawing of the state tree of South Carolina. I thought I had drawn a pretty good cabbage palmetto, but the teacher felt differently and failed me.

It would have been nice to have an objective and consistent scoring system for this assignment. Taking this a step further, an objective and consistent scoring system would be useful for many aspects of our lives, including data modeling. The quality of the data model directly impacts many characteristics of the resulting application, including stability and data quality. Therefore, because a good data model can lead to a good application, and similarly, a bad data model can lead to a bad application, we need an objective way of measuring what is good or bad about the model. After reviewing hundreds of data models, I formalized the criteria I have been using into what I call the data model scorecard.

The scorecard is shown in table 11.1. There are points associated with each of the 10 categories. You can vary the category scores based on the importance to your organization, as long as the total of the all the points remains 100.

Table 11.1 Data model scorecard

#	Question	Total score	Model score	%	Comments
1	Is the model correct?	15			
2	Is the model complete?	15			
3	Is the model structurally sound?	15			
4	Does the model make use of flexible structures where appropriate?	10			
5	Does the model follow naming standards?	5			
6	Is the model properly arranged?	5			
7	Are the definitions useful?	10			
8	Is the physical data model optimized for space and performance?	10			
9	Is the model consistent with the enterprise?	5			
10	Does the metadata match the data?	10			
	TOTAL SCORE	100			

Each of the 10 categories has a total score that relates to the value your organization places on the question. Remember, just as in any assessment, the total must be 100. The model score column contains the results of how a particular model scored. For example, if a model received 10 on "Is the model correct?" then that is what would go in this column. The % column stores the model score in category divided by the total score in category. For example, receiving 10 out of 15 would lead to 66%. The comments column contains any pertinent information to explain the score in more details or to capture the action items on what is required to fix the model. The last row contains the total score, and this can be tallied up or averaged for each of the columns to arrive at a overall score.

Nine of the 10 categories can be applied to all three types of models: subject area, logical, and physical. There is one category that is only pertinent for the physical data model and this is category 8. If you are grading a model that is not a physical data model, I would recommend removing 8 from the scorecard and reallocating the 10 points across the other categories according to what is most valuable to your organization.

The scorecard has three main characteristics that make it an invaluable tool:

- **The scorecard starts by assuming the model is perfect.** As analysts, at times we immediately notice what is wrong. This can lead to quickly pointing out the negative in designs, which can make us blind to what is good in the model and can cause conflict among project team members. The scorecard starts off with a perfect score of 100, and then we subtract from this score points from categories where we identify areas for improvement.

- **The scorecard is objective and externally-defined.** I have participated in model reviews where modelers take the review personally and comments take the form of "I don't like what you did here…" or "You are still not getting this structure right…" We need to step back from the 'I' and 'You', and critique the model with an external and objective perspective. Team rapport remains in tact as you as the reviewer are not criticizing their model, but rather this objective and external scale believes there are areas for improvement.

- **The scorecard is easy to apply and standardize.** The scorecard was designed for even those new to modeling to critique their own models and models of their colleagues. It should be incorporated into a methodology as a final checkpoint before the model is considered complete.

Here are the 10 categories that are described in detail in the following sections:

1. How well does the model capture the requirements?
2. How complete is the model?
3. How structurally sound is the model?
4. How well does the model leverage generic structures?
5. How well does the model follow naming standards?
6. How well has the model been arranged for readability?
7. How good are the definitions?
8. How well has real world context been incorporated into the model?
9. How consistent is the model with the enterprise?
10. How well does the metadata match the data?

1. How well does the model capture the requirements?

This is the "correctness" category. That is, we need to understand the content of what is being modeled. This can be the most difficult of all 10 categories to grade, the reason being that we really need to understand how the business works and what the business wants from their application. If we are modeling a *sales data mart*, for example, we need to understand both how the invoicing process works in our company, as well as what reports and queries will be needed to answer key sales questions from the business.

What makes this category even more challenging is the possibility that perhaps the business requirements are not well-defined, or differ from verbal requirements, or keep changing usually with the scope expanding instead of contracting. We need to ensure our model represents the data requirements, as the costs can be devastating if there is even a slight difference between what was required and what was delivered. Besides not delivering what was expected is the potential that the IT/business relationship will suffer.

Here are a few of the red flags I look for to validate this first category. By *red flag*, I mean something that stands out as a violation of this category. Each of these affect the total point score for the category and must be addressed to receive a perfect score.

Modeling the wrong perspective. Usually one of my first questions when reviewing a data model is to identify why it is being produced in the first place. Remember the "purpose" discussion from chapter 9? What are goals of the model and who is the audience whose needs should be met with this model? For example, if there is a need for analysts to understand a business area such as manufacturing, a model capturing how an existing application views the manufacturing area will not usually be acceptable. Although in reality it is likely both the manufacturing application and business processes will work very similar, they will be differences and at times and these differences can be large especially in the case of ERP packages.

Data elements with formats different from industry standards. For example, a five-character Social Security number or a six-character phone number. This is a red flag that can be identified without much knowledge of the content of the model.

Incorrect cardinality. Assume the business rule is "We hire only applicants who completed a master's degree." Does the model in fig. 11.1 show this?

Fig. 11.1 Cardinality red flag

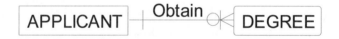

No. It shows that each *applicant* can obtain zero, one or many *degrees*. Yet the cardinality allows an *applicant* to have zero degrees, which violates our business rule. Also, *degree* includes all possible types of degrees, with a master's degree being just one of these. So if Bob has only a bachelor's degree, that would not satisfy our business rule.

We will need to subtype to enforce the specific rule to master's degree, as shown in fig. 11.2.

Fig. 11.2 Cardinality now matches business rule

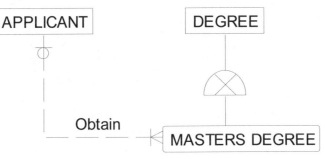

In fig. 11.2, each *applicant* must have at least one *master's degree*, which supports our business rule.

Notice in the corrected example that we needed to use a dotted line instead of a solid line. That is, a non-identifying relationship instead of an identifying relationship. The reason for this is that when we use subtyping, the primary key of the subtype must be the same as the primary key of its supertype. *Master's degree* must have the same primary key as *degree* and therefore the foreign key from *applicant* must not be part of the primary key of *master's degree*.

As a proactive measure to improve the correctness of the data model, I have found the following techniques to be very helpful:

- **Normalization.** Normalization forces us to understand the rules behind what is actually being modeled. We need to ask many questions, and the more we know the more our model will accurately support the business rules.
- **Use abstraction when in doubt.** If the requirements are not known or are incomplete, abstracting allows us to accommodate the unknown by using generic structures. For example, if we don't know and can't confirm whether a customer has a main phone number, fax number, and mobile number; or whether they have a office number and home number, a simple abstract structure containing *customer phone* and *customer phone type* would accommodate all situations.
- **Understand similar situations.** I was once able to leverage knowledge I had about the ordering process for a candy company while modeling how products were ordered for a health care provider. The products were completely different yet the process and a majority of the information were the same.
- **Require stakeholder signoff.** Make sure your users are committed and supportive of the design by requiring their signoff upon model completion. They will take the review much more seriously and be more supportive of the resulting design. If the

analysts would prefer not to look at the model, a popular technique is to validate the model through other mediums such as reports, screens, and prototypes.

2. How complete is the model?

This question ensures the scope of the model matches the scope of the requirements. You can validate the correctness category and this category in parallel, as the red flags and pro-active measures are very similar. For completeness, we need to make sure the scope of the project and model match, as well as ensuring all the necessary metadata on the model is populated.

If the scope of the model is greater than the requirements, we have a situation known as "scope creep." This means that we are planning on delivering more than what was originally required. This may not necessarily be a bad thing, as long as this additional scope has been factored into the project plan. If the model scope is less than the requirements, we will be leaving information out of the resulting application, usually leading to an enhancement or "phase 2" shortly after the application is in production.

Regarding metadata, there are certain types that tend to get overlooked when modeling, such as definitions, stewardship (defined by Anne Marie Smith as "responsibility without authority"), and alternate keys. These types of metadata along with ones that are mandatory parts of our model such as data element name and format information need to be checked for completeness in this category.

Here are a few of the red flags I look for to validate this category:

Information on reports or requirements specifications that do not appear in the model. Are they missing from the model because they are easily derivable in the application? Did we receive oral commitment that they were not needed even though in the documentation it specified that they were needed? Were they simply forgotten from the model? Make sure everything is in writing and agreed to by the business. This reduces surprises during development and implementation phases.

Missing or additional states. One of the more popular red flags for completeness concerns states. A state is a recognizable milestone in the life cycle of a business concept. For example, an order goes through the following states: open, dropped, shipped, received, returned, and so on. It is important to be aware of the states that exist as it will help us make sure we have the right set. We don't want to bring in more than we need because it can cause security, data quality, and performance issues. Once I almost brought in research products into a sales BI application. This sensitive state identifies products to be released to the market in the coming months. Likewise, we don't want to bring in less than we need because we won't make the users very happy. It is not uncommon to leave a state off a model because of definition differences or lack of knowledge that the state even exists. Would a marketing BI solution need prospects or only current customers, for example?

Missing alternate keys when using surrogate keys. There needs to be something "real" to tie to so that the development team can code successfully add from change logic, and so that the business can retrieve a specific entity instance using the data element keys they are accustomed to using. For example *customer* might be identified by the surrogate key customer identifier. Yet when a new customer record is received in the system or when a business person wants to run a report on a specific customer, which data elements are being used to retrieve that customer? This is usually the alternate key.

Missing definitions. This is an all too common red flag that is easy to detect and important to repair, especially for BI applications where the definitions can be critical for knowledge workers to make informed decisions.

As a proactive measure to improve the completeness of the data model, I have found it helpful to apply the techniques mentioned under correctness plus:

- Identify any ambiguously defined terms and clarify any areas of confusion. This is often around the topic of states.
- **Have all documented issues been addressed?** Make sure there are not outstanding issues that would compromise the completeness of the model.
- **Use a metadata checklist.** I believe in providing project teams with a complete checklist of the types of information you expect them to capture during the analysis and design phases. Such a list provides "no excuses" when you identify gaps. At one point I played a game called "metadata bingo," in which we identified a superset of the types of metadata that were of interest to our department. *The Data Modeler's Workbench* has an entire chapter dedicated to this checklist.

3. How structurally sound is the model?

This is the "Data Modeling 101" category. That is, this category ensures that the model follows good design principles. We don't need to necessarily understand the content of the model to score this category. Many of the potential problems from this category are quickly and automatically flagged by our modeling and database tools. Examples include prohibiting having two data elements with the same exact name in the same entity, a null data element in a primary key, and certain reserved words in data element and entity names.

Here are a few of the red flags I look for to validate this category:

Empty entities. Despite the strangeness of this statement, I have seen entities containing zero data elements more than I would like to admit. This is sometimes due to accidentally forward engineering (converting from the model to database tables) entities that were designed as legends in the model or placeholders for the next phase of the project.

Improper use of surrogate keys. This includes over or under-utilizing surrogate keys. Over-utilizing would involve adding a surrogate key to an associative entity purely for the sake of consistency. An example of under-utilizing surrogate keys would be deciding to uses a large and inefficient composite primary key instead of a surrogate key.

Inappropriate multivalued data elements. Having a data element called *customer name* that contains both first and last name, for example.

Relationships that don't have foreign keys correctly propagated. Also known as a partial-key relationship, it occurs when the modeler would like only a subset of the parent's primary key to appear in the child entity as a foreign key.

Data elements with the same name yet different formats. For example, *person telephone number* is 20 characters long in one entity and 10 characters long in another.

Circular and redundant relationships. A circular relationship is a catch-22. That is, to do A, we need to do B, To do B, we need to do C. To do C, we need to do A. Therefore, we are stuck. An example of a circular relationship appears in fig. 11.3.

Fig. 11.3 Circular relationship

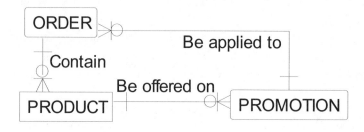

Each *order* can contain zero, one, or many *products*.
Each *product* can be offered on zero, one, or many *promotions*.
Each *promotion* can be applied to zero, one, or many *orders*.

Because these three entities are connected with identifying relationships, there is no way we can create any entity instance without having at least another one other entity instance already in place. In other words, we become stuck. We are stuck because we can't create an *order* without a *promotion*, yet a *promotion* requires an *order* before it can be created.

A redundant relationship is one that is derivable from other relationships on the model. See fig. 11.4.

Fig. 11.4 Redundant relationship

Each *order* can contain zero, one, or many *products*.
Each *product* can be offered on zero, one, or many *promotions*.

Therefore we know the order for a given promotion without explicitly showing the relationship between *order* and *promotion*. If we are building a BI application, showing this redundant relationship might make sense if it improves performance and navigation.

As a proactive measure to improve the structure of the data model, I have found the following techniques to be very helpful:

- **Make sure each data element's format matches the rest of the data element's metadata.** Many times we can identify something structurally incorrect when the formatting of a data element does not seem right, such as a 40-character state code or a 10-character last name.
- **Put your model down and come back to it the next day.** Modeling is one of those activities that at times require simply working on something else for a while and then coming back to your model. I have had modeling revelations a few minutes after picking up a model, whereas a day earlier I was pulling hairs out trying to come up with a creative solution.
- **Try Validator.** This is a piece of software that Computer Associates markets that checks a data model against about 50 criteria. I have found it very useful to identify minor structural inconsistencies that would be too time consuming and difficult for me to check manually. For example, this tool identifies when two or more data elements with the same name have different formats across entities.

4. How well does the model leverage generic structures?

This question ensures the correct level of abstraction is applied on the model. One of the most powerful tools a data modeler has at their disposal is abstraction, the ability to increase the types of information a design can accommodate using abstract structures. Going from Customer Location to a more generic Location for example, allows the design to more easily handle other types of locations, such as warehouses and distribution centers.

There are two red flags I look for to validate this category:

Under abstracting. If I see on a data model many entities that are similar in nature, I would question whether abstraction would be appropriate. Factoring into this equation is the type of application we are building. A BI application for example, would rarely contain abstract structures while a data warehouse which requires flexibility and longevity would be a good candidate for abstraction.

Over abstracting. Likewise, if I see too much abstraction on a model, I would question whether the "value" factor in abstraction discussed earlier has really been considered.

As a proactive measure to ensure the correct level of abstraction, I find myself constantly asking the "value" question. That is, if a structure is abstracted, can we actually reap the benefits some time in the not so distant future?

5. How well does the model follow naming standards?

Correct and consistent naming standards are extremely helpful for knowledge transfer and integration. New team members who are familiar with similar naming conventions on other projects will avoid the time to learn a new set of naming standards. Efforts to bring together information from multiple systems will be less painful if the data elements are named consistently across projects. This category focuses on naming standard structure, abbreviations, and syntax.

Structure includes the components of a name. A popular standard for data element structure is one Subject Area, zero, one, or many Modifiers, and one Class Word. We know from an earlier discussion that a subject area is a concept that is basic and critical to the business. A modifier qualifies this subject area and a class word as previously mentioned is the high-level domain for a data element. Examples of class words are Quantity, Amount, Code, and Date. Enforcing a naming standard on Gross Sales for example, would require us to accurately identify the class word, such as Gross Sales Amount. Enforcing a naming standard on Name would require us to accurately identify the subject area and modifiers, such as *customer last name*.

An abbreviations list should be used to name each logical and physical term. Organizations should have a process in place for efficiently creating new abbreviations if a term cannot be found on a list. The process should be carefully managed to prevent different abbreviations being created for the same or similar term, and for creating the same abbreviation for completely different terms.

Syntax includes whether the term should be plural or singular, whether hyphens spaces, or Hungarian (i.e. initial upper case such as CustomerLastName) should be used, and case includes whether the terms should be all upper case, initial upper case, all lower case.

Here are a few of the red flags I look for to validate this category:

- Entity names that sound more like data elements, such as Customer Type Code.
- Data element names that don't follow the structure one Subject Area, zero, one, or many Modifiers, and one Class Word such as Gross Sales and Name.
- Inconsistent syntax, such as Customer Last Name, CUSTOMER FIRST NAME and customer_middle_initial_name.

As a proactive measure to improve the naming standards on the data model, I have found the following techniques to be very helpful:

- **Publish your naming standards <u>clearly</u> and <u>succinctly</u> in a format that is <u>easily accessible.</u>** Ideally, keep your naming standards to a maximum of a few pages and make it very easy to read and user-friendly. Also publish it on Web sites, shared drives, and so on, to make it as easy as possible for people to reference.
- **Look for opportunities to automate as much of the abbreviations process as possible.** For example, there are some software tools out there that will let you import an abbreviations list and then automatically apply the abbreviations to data element and entity names. This can save much time and reduce human errors.
- **Apply naming conventions as early as possible in the life cycle.** The earlier you apply or validate naming standards, the greater the chance the design and development teams will be more receptive to make the changes. After there is code written against the data elements it can be much more work to change the data element names.
- **Have rules about when to "Grandfather" older names.** When I notice data element names that don't follow standards, it is possible that different or older naming standards might have been used. In situations like this I prefer to have consistent and "wrong" names rather than inconsistency with some percentage of the names following current naming standards. For example, I would rather have CUST_LAST_NAME appear consistently throughout the model, instead of having CUST_LAST_NAME and CUST_LST_NAM appear within the same model.

6. How well has the model been arranged for readability?

This question checks to make sure the model is visually easy to follow. This question is definitely the least important category. However, if your model is hard to read you may not accurately address the more important categories on the scorecard. Readability needs to be considered at a model, entity, data element, and relationship level.

At a model level, I like to see a large model broken into smaller logical pieces. I also search for the "heart" of the model. That is, upon looking at a data model, which part of the model are your eyes naturally attracted toward? This tends to be an entity or entities with many relationships to other entities, similar to the hub on a bicycle tire with many spokes to the outside rim of the tire. This "heart" needs to be carefully positioned so that the reader can identify it early on and use this as a starting point to walk through the rest of the model.

At an entity level, I like to see child entities below parent entities. Child entities being on the many side of the relationship, and parent entities on the one side of the relationship. So if an *order* contains many *order lines*, *order line* should appear below *order*.

At a data element level, I like to see some logic applied regarding the placement of data elements within an entity. For example, on reference entities such as *customer* and *employee*, it is more readable to have the data elements listed in an order that makes sense for someone starting at the beginning of the entity and working down sequentially. For example, *city name*, then *state name*, then *postal code*. For transaction entities such as *order* and *claim*, I have found it more readable to group the data elements into class words, such as all amount data elements grouped together.

At a relationship level, I avoid crossing relationship lines or lines going through unrelated entities. I also look for missing or incomplete relationship labels, if labels are appropriate on the model. The larger the model, the less useful it is to display labels as the extra verbiage can make the model harder to read.

Here are a few of the red flags I look for to validate this category:
- Child entities above Parent entities.
- No logic or poor logic in data element order. For example, if the data elements are alphabetized within an entity, so that *customer middle initial name* appears after *customer last name*.
- Relationship lines crossing each other or through unrelated entities.
- Difficulty finding the "heart" of the model.

As a proactive measure to improve the readability of the data model, I have found the most important technique is to actually put yourself in your audiences' shoes. That is, if you were the person who needs to completely understand the model, how would you like to see it arranged to make it as easy to read as possible?

7. How good are the definitions?

As mentioned previously, good definitions support the data model diagram and remove doubt about the contents of data elements and the relationships between entities. A good definition has clarity, completeness, and accuracy. Clarity means that a reader can understand the meaning of a term by reading the definition only once. Completeness ensures the definition is at the appropriate level of detail, and that it includes all the necessary components such as derivations and examples. Accuracy focuses on having a definition that totally matches what the term means, and is consistent with the rest of the business.

Here are a few of the red flags I look for to validate this category:

- Entity definitions that only describe what the entity contains, such as this definition for *customer*: "Customer contains last name, first name, and address."
- Data elements definitions that provide no additional value and restate the obvious. For example, Associate Identifier's definition is *"The identifier for the associate"*.
- Definitions that appear to be wrong or inconsistent with other information we know about the data element. For example, Customer Shoe Size is defined as *"The middle name of the customer."*
- Derived data elements missing an explanation of the derivation.

As a proactive measure to improve the definitions associated with the data model, make sure each definition is clear, complete, and accurate. Similar to the "putting yourself in your audience's shoes" statement made under the readability category, ask yourself whether somebody from outside the department or area being modeled can easily understand the data element or entity based on your definition.

8. How well has real world context been incorporated into the model?

This is the only category of the scorecard that pertains to just one type of data model: the physical data model. Here we consider important factors to an application's success, such as response time, storage space, backup and recovery, security, reporting tool needs, and so on.

Here are a few of the red flags I look for to validate this category:

- **Too much being done by the reporting tool.** In a BI application, if a report is taking two hours to run then the reporting tool might be doing too much of the work. There could be very complex calculations being done "on the fly".
- **Long null data elements appearing toward the top of the table on a physical data model.** Long null variable length string fields should be moved toward the end of each entity. There is a good chance the data element will not be filled in or be shorter than the maximum field length. This can save space at the end of each record, which is often a factor when we are dealing with very large tables. For example *consumer comments text* defined as a null 255-character string most likely will save space by appearing as the last data element in an entity instead of the first.
- **No partitioning.** Both vertical and horizontal partitioning can be effective techniques to save space and increase retrieval, update, delete, and create speeds.

- **No or little indexing.** For example, no index on *month name* when this data element is used often in selection criteria.
- **Denormalization chosen incorrectly over views.** In all but two situations which were described earlier, views should be chosen over denormalization to maintain model integrity and flexibility.

As a proactive measure to improve the physical data model, I have found the following techniques to be very helpful:

- **Become familiar with what your database and reporting tools like and don't like.** Not how the reporting tool works, rather an understanding of the ideal structures for a particular reporting tool.
- **Know when to use materialized views versus regular views versus letting a reporting tool do the work.** This is a tough decision but depending on volumes and usage, materialized views are increasingly the preferred choice.
- **Be very selective with denormalization and use the appropriate type.** Decide whether FUBES, repeating groups, standard, and so on, are most appropriate.
- **Are the physical structures easily navigated?** In BI applications where users have direct access, it is important to have structures that are user-friendly and understandable.

9. How consistent is the model with the enterprise?

Does this model complement the "big picture"? This question ensures information is represented in a broad and consistent context. The structures that appear in a data model should be consistent in terminology and usage to structures that appear in related data models, and with the enterprise model if one exists. This way there will be consistency across projects. If no enterprise model exists, I look for widely accepted existing models for comparison, ERP models if they are accessible and intelligible, or universal models which are models that are built for a particular industry or function.

Here are a few of the red flags I look for to validate this category:

- **Synonyms.** "Project XYZ calls it *client*, but the enterprise calls it *customer*"
- **Homonyms.** Homonyms are words with the same name but have different meanings. Homonyms can be very difficult to detect, as sometimes differences can be very subtle. Knowing the states a concept goes through can help detect and correct these situations. For example, a marketing department might use the term *customer* to refer to prospects, whereas the accounting department might only consider organizations that have already made a purchase to be considered a customer. Both Project XYZ and the enterprise call it *customer*, but it means two different things.
- **Format differences.** If there is a data element on your model that is a longer length than on other models, the consequences are usually less disastrous than if

your data element is shorter than on other data models and truncated data is possible.

As a proactive measure to improve consistency, I have found the following techniques to be very helpful:

- **Leverage an enterprise model.** If one does not exist, it does not take too much time and minimal pain to build one at a subject area level.
- **Reuse as much as possible from similar models.** This includes subject matter and common sets of data elements. Subject matter meaning if you are designing a customer area, perhaps that specific area of customer has already been modeled and can be copied into your model. Common sets of data elements meaning if there is a standard way of representing phone numbers or address for example, you can copy these directly into your model.
- **Make friends.** I have found those with in-depth knowledge of a specific area and those with broad business understanding to be invaluable to ensure consistency within my model.

10. How well does the metadata match the data?

This question ensures the model and the actual data that will be stored within the resulting tables are consistent with each other. This category determines how well the data elements and their rules match reality. This might be very difficult to do early in a project's life cycle, but the earlier the better so you can avoid future surprises which can be much more costly.

Here are a few of the red flags I look for to validate this category:

- **Blatant errors.** These are situations when the data is obviously completely different than what is implied by the data element's name and definition. For example, *customer eye color text* contains the customer's shoe size.
- **Linking data elements not linking.** A linking data element is a data element that is a foreign key to an entity in a different subject area. For instance, *item identifier* in *order* is a linking data element back to *item*. *Student number* in *registration* is a linking data element back to *student*. These are difficult to detect, but one quickly appreciates how much frustration and wasted time can be caused by these linking data elements if they don't link as expected.
- **Length errors.** For example, a data element 2,000 characters long in which at most only the first 10 characters are populated. Or worse yet, a data element five characters long that appears to contain truncated data.

As a proactive measure to ensure the data matches the metadata, I have found the following techniques to be very helpful:

- **Complete the data quality validation template.** This is a spreadsheet I use that contains the metadata in one set of columns, the results of data checking in another set of columns, and validation by a business expert in the final set of columns. Validation by a business expert is essential to ensuring there is a data/metadata match. This template can be downloaded from www.stevehoberman.com. You can also read chapter 5 in *The Data Modeler's Workbench.*
- **Do as early as possible to avoid costly surprises later.** Sometimes it can be difficult to get the data, or we can receive access only to a limited set of data.
- **Give linking data element priority.**

Exercise 11.1

Apply the scorecard to a data model that you are currently working on or one that has been recently completed. Customize the scorecard if necessary.

CHAPTER 12: Top three most frequently asked modeling questions

These questions have been asked during my modeling courses and in discussion panels. If you have a question that is not listed here, feel free to e-mail it to me at me@stevehoberman.com.

How do I keep my modeling skills sharp?

Look for every opportunity to model or participate in the analysis and modeling process, even outside the traditional roles of a data modeler. The more roles we play around the modeling space, the greater our modeling skills become. For example, after modeling for a number of years, I decided to try development. As a developer, I became one of the customers of the data model, looking at the model with a different eye from that of the modeler. I became able to anticipate questions such as these in my design:

- How can I efficiently populate this structure with an extract, transform, and load (ETL) tool?
- Where are opportunities where things can break and how can this be efficiently addressed structurally?
- How can we extract data out as rapidly as possible for reporting?

Thinking of these questions during my modeling helped me become more of a practical data modeler. It broadened my view on the physical data model, and when I returned to modeling, I anticipated many of the questions I knew the developers needed to know on the physical data model.

This may sound geeky, but I also find myself modeling forms and documents outside work that I encounter in my personal life. For example, I might sketch the data model for a menu while waiting to order food in a restaurant. I remember looking at the label of a bottle of prescription medicine and being surprised how concatenated and multivalued some of the fields were that were printed on the label. I therefore started sketching what the ideal data model would be that could store all this prescription information and correct some of these data problems.

There are some excellent books to read and websites that contain newsletters and other valuable information that I've listed under the Suggested Reading section. Also, if you visit my Web site, www.stevehoberman.com, you can sign up for my design challenge discussion list. I send out frequent modeling scenarios to everyone on the list, and then I receive a few responses on how to overcome the challenge. I consolidate everyone's responses (including my own) and send them back out to the group. There are over a thousand people who receive these challenges, so get your e-mail address added to the list!

There are conferences, courses, and data organizations that keep us in touch with the industry. The Data Warehousing Institute (www.tdwi.org) offers some in-depth courses and conferences on data modeling and business intelligence. DAMA (www.dama.org) has a very large annual conference; there are also many local DAMA chapters with monthly meetings. It's a great way to network. There are also modeling tool user groups such as the user group for the Erwin modeling tool (www.causergroups.com). I belong to the New York Erwin User Group and find it a good forum for sharing ideas and learning more about modeling and Erwin.

What is the best data modeling tool?

This is one of the favorite barroom topics among data modelers. Picture a darkly lit tavern where a few unshaven data modelers are at the bar with drinks in their hands. "Erwin is the best modeling tool on the market!" is immediately rebutted with "ER Studio is better and will always be better!" The shouts continue.

In the bigger context of software development, it doesn't really matter which tool is used, as long as the finished product is accessible and easily maintainable. The newest released features in one modeling tool give that tool a temporary advantage until competition catches up with these features, adds new ones, and then temporarily has an advantage in the marketplace. Just make sure that the tool you choose supports metadata capture (a place to put definitions), forward engineering (creating database tables from the model), reverse engineering (creating a model from database tables), and rubber banding (the ability to automatically redraw lines when the entity boxes are moved). This last requirement may sound like more of a luxury than a necessity, but I once reviewed a data model with several hundred entities completed in PowerPoint! You can imagine the model maintenance when new entities and data elements needed to be added.

I have used the Erwin modeling tool a very long time (since version 2.0) and have found a lot of the more advanced features such as Complete Compare and support for naming abbreviations to be very helpful. I have also heard that ER Studio also has a lot of great features and also has a very robust macro language to add your own features. If you are in the process of deciding which tool such as these two or others are right for your organization, ask for free demos or download them from the vendor websites.

What is the future role of the data modeler?

There will always be new systems to build, and therefore I believe there will always be analyst and modeler skills required. There is a trend, however, to buying Enterprise Resource Planning (ERP) software that I think will continue indefinitely. This trend creates an additional opportunity for the modeler, as someone who now needs to be the translator or detective in figuring out what makes these systems tick and capture and explain how our existing systems relate to this new system. For example, recently I was asked to model a subset of SAP/R3 that manages raw materials to explain to the business the vast number of tables required for consideration in an archiving strategy. This was not the typical role for a data modeler but I was definitely able to use my skills to add value. I therefore think in the future, the data modeler will play a number of non-traditional roles including an ERP Data Analyst.

Suggested Reading

Books

Adelman S., Moss L., Abai M. 2005. *Data Strategy*. Boston, MA: Addison-Wesley Publishing Company.

Eckerson, W. 2005. Performance Dashboards: Measuring, Monitoring, and Managing Your Business. New York: John Wiley & Sons, Inc.

Hay, D. 1995. *Data Modeling Patterns*. Dorset House Publishing Company, Incorporated.

Hoberman, S. 2001. *The Data Modeler's Workbench*. New York: John Wiley & Sons, Inc.

Imhoff C., Galemmo, N., Geiger, J. 2003. *Mastering Data Warehouse Design: Relational and Dimensional Techniques*. New York: John Wiley & Sons, Inc.

Marco D., Jennings M. 2004. *Universal Metadata Models*. New York: John Wiley & Sons, Inc.

Marco, D. 2000. *Building and Managing the Metadata Repository: A Full Lifecycle Guide*. New York: John Wiley & Sons, Inc.

Kimball R., Reeves L, Ross M., Thornthwaite, W. 1998. The Data Warehouse Lifecycle Toolkit: Expert Methods for Designing, Developing, and Deploying Data Warehouses. New York: John Wiley & Sons, Inc.

Silverston, L.2001. The Data Model Resource Book, Revised Edition, Volume 1, A Library of Universal Data Models For All Enterprises. New York: John Wiley & Sons, Inc.

Silverston, L.2001. The Data Model Resource Book, Revised Edition, Volume 2, A Library of Universal Data Models For Industry Types. New York: John Wiley & Sons, Inc.

Simsion G., Witt G. 2005. *Data Modeling Essentials, Third Edition*. San Francisco: Morgan Kaufmann Publishers.

Web sites

www.dama.org – Conferences, chapter information, and articles.

www.debtechint.com – Great public and onsite training courses.

www.dmreview.com – I use the article search mechanism often.

www.ewsolutions.com – Quarterly newsletter containing informative articles on metadata, data warehousing, and data modeling.

www.stevehoberman.com – Add your e-mail address to the Design Challenge list to receive modeling puzzles.

www.tdan.com – In-depth quarterly newsletter. I visit this site very often to read the current newsletter or search the archives.

www.tdwi.org – Great conferences, seminars, and white papers.

www.teradata.com – Great white papers, even if your organization does not currently use Teradata.

Quick Order Form
Data Modeling Made Simple
A Practical Guide for Business & IT Professionals

Email orders: orders@technicspub.com

Web orders: www.technicspub.com

Postal orders: Technics Publications
                 PO Box 161
                 Bradley Beach, NJ 07720

Name:_____

Address:_____

City:_____State:_____Zip:_____

Telephone:_____

Email address: _____

Shipping by air
US: $4.00
International: $9.00

Please pay by check or money order if ordering through the mail. Online orders can use credit cards.